Fortress Fremantle

Its Lost Sub & Contribution to World War II

D1211281

TIM BALDOCK

FORTRESS FREMANTLE

Published by Tim Baldock for
Baldock Family Trust

© Tim Baldock 2018

First printed June 2018 by
Lightning Source

Creator: Baldock, Tim. (author)
Title: Fortress Fremantle
ISBN: 978-0-6483649-0-0 (black and white)
Subject: Military History - Naval

Cover photo: *Preparing submarines
for operations in Fremantle Harbour.*

Images in Creative Commons
unless otherwise specified

Artwork and Design by
Green Hill Publishing

This book is dedicated to the memory of
the 84 servicemen aboard the
USS Bullhead *who lost their lives in 1945.*

CONTENTS

INTRODUCTION

The Port of Fremantle played one of the most predominant roles of any Australian port or city during World War II. Not only was it a significant embarkation point, and subsequently the last glimpse of Australia for thousands of servicemen heading overseas to serve their country, it was also one of the most crucial submarine bases of the Second World War. The importance of which was so recognised by the military, that for the duration of the war, most people who resided in the port city had no idea of what was really going on there.

The base was occupied by submarines from the American, British and Dutch navies, who had fled the relentless and inexorable Japanese juggernaut that had swept through the Philippines, Malaya, Singapore, and the Dutch East Indies following the bombing of Pearl Harbour just before Christmas in 1941, which brought the United States into the Second World War alongside Britain and Australia, who had been embroiled in the conflict since the German invasion of Poland in September 1939.

Australia was recognised as an important strategic asset, and in February 1942, the US and British Governments agreed that Australia would become the responsibility of the United States. The Allied force was created specifically to defend the Australian continent. In March 1942, General Douglas MacArthur arrived in Australia after escaping from the Philippines and assumed command of the South West Pacific Area. All Australian combat units in this area were placed under his command, with MacArthur replacing the Australian Chief of Staff as the Australian Government's main source of military advice until the end of the war.

The Japanese Government thought long and hard about an invasion of Australia in early 1942, and one of their most admired Generals, General Yamashita, also known as the Tiger of Malaya, pushed heavily for an aggressive invasion after demonstrating the mettle and endurance of his soldiers who had poured down the Malayan peninsula to conquer the hitherto impregnable 'fortress' of Singapore.

Despite Australia's fear and Yamashita's urgings, the Japanese military ultimately decided against an invasion of Australia primarily due to it being reckoned to be above the Japanese Military's capabilities, plus the difficulties of maintaining and supplying a huge military force over such a vast distance from Japan. Instead, the decision was made to isolate Australia from the United States by capturing Port Moresby in New Guinea, as well as the Solomon Islands. This plan was frustrated by Japans failure to land a blow on the Americans at the Battle of the Coral Sea and was postponed indefinitely following Japan's crushing defeat to the Americans at the Battle of Midway.

Australia continued to fear invasion from Japan though, and continued to bolster the defences of Fremantle, particularly as the importance of the submarine fleet grew. The menace provided by this undersea fleet kept the Captains of both military as well as merchant fleets in a state of constant anxiety when they were on the water. They were acutely aware of the vulnerability of their vessels to a torpedo, and although rarely seen, if a torpedo was detected it was not until the last moment, when it was too late.

The American submarine fleet made up only about 10 percent of the personnel of their World War II navy, yet they managed to inflict catastrophic losses on Japan's merchant fleet, which were unable to effectively counter them, and were crucial to supplying the Island nation that had very few natural resources of its own.

Some of America's most successful submarines were based at Fremantle, including *Flasher* which had an outstanding service record. Eleven American Submarines that were based at Fremantle were lost at sea, and, unfortunately for it, the USS *Bullhead*, the last American ship sunk in World War II, departed on its final and fateful voyage from Fremantle Harbour on 31 July 1945, seven days prior to its sinking.

The impressive defences of 'Fortress Fremantle' included several heavy gun batteries ranging from Swanbourne in the north, to Rockingham and Garden Island in the south, and out to the Oliver Hill gun battery at Rottnest Island, which was affectionately known as the 'gatekeepers' of Fremantle harbour and which would be the first guns in this line of defence to engage approaching targets.

The reality was though, that these guns were virtually as obsolete as the battleships that they would be defending Fremantle against, a fact largely unrecognised at the time. The Pacific Theatre changed the entire strategy of naval warfare. The Battle of the Coral Sea was the first naval battle in which the opposing navies never actually saw each other. This was now the age of the aircraft carrier, a colossal tour de force, which could send its arsenal of planes loaded with bombs and torpedos hundreds of miles ahead of itself and inflict huge damage on opposition naval or land forces. The Battle of Midway really was the turning point of the War in The Pacific, where in a few short hours, Japan lost four of her most significant aircraft carriers, and any chance she had of winning the war went to the bottom of the sea with them.

The once-mighty battleships, which for years had ruled the seas, were now completely vulnerable to air attack and the Admirals were very quickly learning this. Many were learning it the hard way though, such as the British who in early 1942 refused to wait for air cover to protect the *Repulse* and the *Prince of Wales*, which had been sent to Malaya as a show of force and were subsequently destroyed with ease by Japanese aircraft. Even Japan, an early adopter of air power launched from carriers, continued to build some of the biggest battleships ever made until surely enough, these too became victims of the aircraft sent to attack them.

A longstanding passion and interest in military history, plus a realisation of there being little public knowledge on the fortress that Fremantle was - given the significance of its contribution to the eventual Allied victory in World War II, is what inspired me to write *Fortress Fremantle: Its Lost Sub & Contribution to World War II.*

Presented in a condensed yet significant manner, my hope is that people reading this book find it a light, easy to comprehend, factual account of what life was like in Fremantle and surrounding lands during the early 1940's when for a while, Australia stood all alone, in the face of great adversity.

BACKGROUND,
THE PACIFIC WAR

O n 6 August 1945, the *Balao*-class submarine, the USS *Bullhead* (SS-332) had the ignominy of being the last American ship lost in the Second World War. She was the 52nd and final American submarine lost during World War II, sinking with a crew of 84 men on board. That date just happened to coincide with the same day that the first atomic bomb, known as 'Little Boy', was dropped from the *Enola Gay* B-29 Superfortress on the Japanese city of Hiroshima.

The dropping of the atomic bomb did not immediately end the war for Japan. The Americans had been flying bomber squadrons over Japanese cities since the middle of 1944, when their planes were now in range of the Japanese mainland following their island-hopping campaign to retake the Pacific. These bombing raids, which comprised the dropping of high-incendiary and blockbuster bombs on a vast number of Japanese cities, had caused massive destruction and the deaths of countless civilians, and was particularly effective given the wooden construction of many of the buildings.

It was not until three days later, on 9 August, when a second bomb, this one plutonium, and nicknamed 'Fat Man', was dropped on the city of Nagasaki, that the Japanese realised that this new 'super weapon' had changed the nature of war forever. This, along with the Soviet Union's recent declaration of war on Japan, saw Japan announce its surrender just days later, on 15 August. On 2 September it signed the instrument of surrender, effectively ending World War II.

Interestingly, many historians believe that the Japanese were more worried about the Russian invasion of Manchuria than the bombs. In fact, there is little mention of any bombs in Japanese cabinet meetings before their surrender. The bomb was largely the pretext for surrender, when Japan was in fact more worried about Russia. There was never any doubt that Russia would enter the war against Japan; this was agreed to by Stalin at the Teheran Conference in November 1943 and reconfirmed at the Yalta Conference in February 1945, where the Russians committed that they would declare war against the Japanese three months after the surrender of Germany. On 8 May 1945, General Alfred Jodl, Chief of Staff of the German Armed Forces High Command, signed the unconditional surrender documents for all German Forces to the Allies at the Supreme Headquarters, Allied Expeditionary Forces, in Reims, France. Exactly three months later, on 8 August 1945, the Soviet foreign minister, Molotov, informed his Japanese counterpart that the Soviet Union had declared war on the Empire of Japan and that from 9 August, ironically the same day the second bomb was dropped on Nagasaki, the two countries would consider themselves at war. At exactly one minute past midnight, the Soviets launched their invasion on three fronts into Japanese-occupied Manchuria.

The Japanese were very concerned about the Russian entry and potentially facing a war on two fronts. As well as having to deal with the expected American invasion of the Japanese mainland, the Japanese army in Manchuria now found itself facing off against the colossal forces of the Soviet Union. Following their defeat of Germany, the Soviets had been steadily transferring forces and equipment to line the border of Russia and Manchuria prior to launching the attack.

Japan was aware that defeat was inevitable and knew that a surrender to the Russians would almost certainly mean the loss of Sakhalin Island, which the Soviet Union had just invaded, and the Kuril Islands. But more importantly, from the perspective of Japanese prestige, would be the expected loss of the island of Hokkaido to the Soviet Union. Hokkaido was firmly in the Russians' sights, and the Japanese Fifth Area Army which was defending it was significantly under-strength following years of war.

Surprisingly, whilst their cities were being carpet-bombed and obliterated in the process, the Japanese military held off surrendering despite the sufferings of their people, assuming that to end the war America would need to invade the Japanese mainland. This would mean the Japanese forces would be able to inflict heavy casualties at that time and perhaps negotiate more favourable surrender terms.

The bombing of the cities of Japan was conducted in an almost clinical manner by the US Air Force. On 28 November

1944 the first of the long-range bombing occurred from the newly-constructed airfields in the Mariana Islands under the command of American General Curtis LeMay. He merged the XX and the XXI Bomber Commands into the XX Air Force, and immediately went about a systematic bombing campaign. The raids were carried out by huge formations of B-29 Superfortress' which had a massive bombload capacity. The bombers were accompanied by the long-range P-51 Mustang fighters in support, which were now vastly superior to the Japanese Zero fighters and, by that stage of the war, to the relatively lightly-trained Japanese pilots who would attempt to intercept them.

The ability of Japan to build new fighter planes to defend its skies was heavily diminished as well by American bombing of the factories that produced the planes. In addition, nearly all of Japan's best pilots, the highly skilled men who had led raids years earlier on Pearl Harbour, Malaya and Singapore, Midway Island and countless other places of battle, had been killed and simply could not be replaced.

The inability of Japan to replace its air crews later in the war was largely due to the lack of aircraft for training following factory destruction and the wasting of fighter pilots with ability; aircraft were also lost through kamikaze missions which, despite intentions, inflicted less damage overall than could have been achieved by conventional tactics. The general indifference of the Japanese military command to their pilots and soldiers was also a factor.

The difference in treatment of aircrew by the respective belligerents was telling. When an American plane was shot down, enormous effort was placed in the retrieval of the pilot through a combination of aircraft, (primarily Catalina seaplanes), destroyers, patrol boats and submarines. This was partly due to the value that was placed by that society on human life, but more important was the potential for that rescued airman to live to fly another day, minimising expense and time in retraining someone else. Japan, on the other hand, had a lower regard for its pilots and virtually no sea rescue operation existed; shot-down pilots who, if rescued, could have flown again and potentially inflict future damage and casualties, were simply left to perish in the Pacific.

The cities of Hiroshima and Nagasaki could perhaps consider themselves a little unlucky to have been the recipients of the devastating new weapons of war introduced by the United States, as they were among a handful of potential cities that had been identified as atomic bomb targets. Before LeMay began his air campaign to destroy Japan's cities he had identified up to 60 medium-to-large cities that he felt needed to be destroyed. And his huge fire-bombing formations certainly did not let him down with regards to the level of destruction they were capable of unleashing through their incendiary attacks.

Although falling into this category of 60 by way of their size, Hiroshima and Nagasaki, along with the cities of Kokura and Niigata, had been left pretty well untouched during the war. This had their citizens wondering when their time might come, but it also had the effect of causing the Japanese military chiefs to scratch their heads wondering why they had been spared this long into the war.

The reason they were left untouched was because it was going to be from these four cities that the final targets would eventually be chosen. The US War Department had advised that it should be possible to use the first atomic bomb shortly after 1 August, depending on the weather, and almost certainly before the tenth. On 25 July, LeMay's superior, General Carl Spaatz, who had overall command of the US Army's Strategic Air Force in the Pacific, received written orders for dropping the two bombs on Japan, approved in Potsdam by Henry Stimson, US Secretary of War, and General George Marshall. It is not clear whether President Truman saw the document containing these orders but it hardly mattered; the issue of the orders was largely a formality. The directive stipulated: 'The 509 Composite Group, Twentieth Air Force, will deliver its first special bomb as soon as weather will permit visual bombing after about 3 August 1945 on one of the targets: Hiroshima, Kokura, Niigata and Nagasaki ... additional bombs will be delivered on the above targets as soon as made ready by the project staff'.

The American Major General, Leslie Groves, who oversaw the Manhattan project which built the bombs and had the role of administering and controlling the project and reporting directly to Stimson, had a preference for the first bomb to be dropped on the Japanese city of Kyoto, which was not included in the group of potential target cities. Kyoto had strong cultural significance for the people of Japan and was the Imperial capital of Japan for more than a thousand years before the capital was moved in 1868 to the city of Edo, and subsequently renamed Tokyo. Groves believed that dropping the bomb on the city with this ancient connection would have the most devastating effect on the morale of the people. Stimson was infuriated to learn of this decision by Groves and he hastened a signal to

Washington vetoing the General's choice. His rationale, as communicated to President Truman, was that the destruction of such a cultural icon would not do a lot to improve the standing of America in the eyes of the Japanese people. He suggested that sparing Kyoto should ensure 'a sympathetic Japan towards the United States in case there should be aggression by Russia in Manchuria'.

So, on 6 August 1945, with favourable weather conditions above it, the world's first deployed atomic bomb was detonated over the city of Hiroshima. The explosion wiped out 90 percent of the city and immediately killed 80,000 people; tens of thousands more would later die of radiation exposure. Meanwhile, thousands of kilometres away in the Java Sea, another significant event was occurring.

A downed US airman awaits rescue.

USS *BULLHEAD*

The USS *Bullhead* left the Port of Fremantle, Western Australia, one of the world's biggest submarine bases during the Second World War, for her final patrol into the waters of the Java Sea on 31 July 1945.

The *Bullhead* (SS-332) was laid down on 21 October 1943 at Groton, Connecticut by the Electric Boat Company. She was launched on 16 July 1944 and commissioned on 4 December 1944 under the command of Walter T Griffith. Griffith was a highly experienced commander and he had had significant experience operating submarines in the war so far. In November 1943, in what was one of the US Navy's most outstanding months for submarine warfare, Griffith's own submarine, *Bowfin*, along with 30 other submarines sank a record 62 Japanese ships, earning Griffith the award of a Navy Cross and the *Bowfin* a Presidential Unit Citation.

Bullhead undertook a 'shakedown cruise' which is where the performance of a ship is tested before entering service, and this was conducted in the waters of Narragansett Bay, which is a large body of water located on the north side of Rhode Island Sound and a common testing ground for vessels built in nearby Connecticut.

On 9 January 1945, *Bullhead* sailed for Key West Florida where she received a further two weeks' additional training before heading off to Panama. She then left the Panama Canal on 11 February and headed for Pearl Harbour, Hawaii. On her first day out of the Panama Canal, disaster almost struck. Whilst conducting a practice dive, the main induction failed to close quickly enough due to low hydraulic pressure and tons of water flooded in before the crew were able to shut it. They managed to save the submarine by shifting ballast, pumping out water and continuing the dive. She proceeded on without incident and arrived in Pearl Harbour on 26 February. Here she undertook repairs and then left on 9 March.

Bullhead paused at Guam about 10 days later to take on fuel and then on 21 March got underway for her first war patrol into the South China Sea. The submarine hunted for targets off Formosa, now Taiwan, however, she was unable to locate any enemy ships. Undeterred she set a course for Hong Kong, and along the way she shelled targets on enemy occupied Pratas Island. While stationed off Hong Kong she provided lifeguard services for downed Allied aviators.

On 8 April, she was mistaken by an American 'Liberator' bomber for an enemy submarine and the plane accidentally bombed her. Fortunately, all the bombs missed, the closest landing 75 yards away, and while shaken by the experience, she sustained no damage. On 16 April, about four miles off the coast of China, *Bullhead* recovered the crew of a downed US aircraft, taking on board the three surviving crew, as well as the bodies of three casualties. The submarine terminated the patrol on 28 April in the Philippines when she arrived safely at the newly-constructed naval base, Subic Bay in Luzon.

Whilst there she undertook a refit, and then spent eight days in training exercises off the coast of Luzon before heading off on her second war patrol on 21 May. This time she teamed up with two other submarines, *Bergall* (SS-320) and *Kraken* (SS-370) to form a wolf pack and conduct a co-ordinated sweep of the Java Sea as well as the Gulf of Siam.

Bullhead entered the patrol area on 25 May but was unable to locate any suitable targets until 30 May, when she made a machine gun attack on a 150 tonne schooner, resulting in the sinking of the vessel. On 4 June, she moved to an area south of Anabas Island but this spot, too, was barren of targets.

On 16 June, she entered the Western end of the Java Sea and on the eighteenth, she located her next victim, a 700 tonne freighter which sank soon after being hit by one of her torpedoes. Later that day the submarine sighted a small convoy comprising two merchant ships and two escort vessels, but she was unable to attack as the ships took shelter along the Java coast. On the morning of 19 June, *Bullhead* engaged in a surface battle with two Japanese subchasers and two picket boats and she took credit for sinking one 700 tonne subchaser and damaging a smaller one of approximately 500 tonnes. Although the Japanese subchasers were not as powerful as the destroyers which undertook that task for the American fleet, they were still formidable opponents and employed at least 36 depth charges with depth charge throwers as well as powerful 25 mm anti-aircraft guns and at least one deck bound cannon. To sink one of these and damage another without receiving damage on itself was a considerable achievement by *Bullhead*. The remaining ships tried to take cover behind a point of land, but *Bullhead* approached the shore and continued firing on them. The encounter finally ended when the submarine had exhausted her supply of 5 inch ammunition for her main gun.

On 25 June, *Bullhead* opened fire with her 40 mm gun on a small Japanese vessel, setting it ablaze and believing it to be sunk. She completed this patrol on 2 July when she arrived and safely moored at Fremantle. Despite claiming to have sunk several vessels, USS *Bullhead* was not officially credited with destroying any Japanese shipping on this patrol. Whilst in the Port of Fremantle she undertook a brief refit and as part of this she received another 5 inch gun. On 31 July she departed Fremantle and began her third patrol. Her mission was to transit the Strait of Lombok and patrol in the Java Sea with several other American and British submarines also operating out of Fremantle.

Bullhead rendezvoused with a Dutch submarine, *O-21*, on 2 August and transferred mail to her. Four days later she reported that she had passed safely through the strait and was now in her patrol area. This was the last time anyone heard word from the USS *Bullhead*, and when all attempts to contact her proved fruitless, on 24 August she was reported overdue and presumed lost.

After the war ended, the US Navy conducted an analysis of Japanese military records and this analysis revealed that Japanese aircraft had located a submarine just off the Bali coast near the northern mouth of Lombok Strait on 6 August 1945, and that a Japanese Air Force plane had attacked and dropped two 500 pound bombs on the target.

The pilot claimed two direct hits and reported seeing a gush of oil, as well as air bubbles at the spot that the target went down. The land surrounding the Lombok Strait is mountainous, and it was presumed that the mountains shortened the submarine's radar range and prevented *Bullhead* from receiving any warning of the plane's impending approach. The submarine went down with the loss of all 84 hands. Her name was struck off the Navy List on 17 September 1945.

Bullhead was the 52nd US submarine lost during World War II. She was also the last US vessel to be lost during the war, sunk on 6 August, probably only hours after the Hiroshima bomb was dropped, and only nine days before the official Japanese surrender ending the world's last horrifying, and truly global, conflict.

USS *Bullhead* leaving port.

Prayer service on board the USS *Bullhead*.

THE FALL OF SINGAPORE

P rior to the dropping of the Hiroshima bomb in August 1945 though, as the now heavily weakened Japanese Imperial Forces went through their death throes, things were very different. In December 1941, following the attack on Pearl Harbour and the invasion of the Philippines and British Malaya, Japan swept all before it as its forces conquered territory with ease.

At the end of January 1942, the Japanese Imperial Army had marched down the Malayan Peninsula and now faced the forces of the British Empire across the Johore Strait on the Island of Singapore. The Japanese forces were led by General Tomoyuki Yamashita, an extremely aggressive and capable General who commanded fierce loyalty and devotion from his soldiers. The British forces comprised soldiers from England, Australia and India, as well as Ghurkas, and were commanded by General Arthur Percival who reported to the overall Commander-in-Chief, Archibald Wavell. These forces numbered close to 100,000 men and Percival was confident that after strengthening the defences of Singapore Island that he would have little trouble defending it from the Japanese whom he knew to have a much smaller number of soldiers.

Singapore was widely regarded by Allied Commanders, and indeed by Winston Churchill, as being impregnable, hence its name of 'Fortress'. Part of this impregnability was based on the five massive 15 inch guns which were stationed on the island covering the vital sea routes that any invading navy would have to negotiate to approach the island. What they failed to allow for was an invading force which did not approach by sea. The Japanese Army, which was heavily outnumbered by the Allies and only totalled some 36,000 men swept down the Malayan peninsula, largely on bicycles. They swiftly arrived at the bottom of the Malayan Peninsula, facing Singapore across the Johore Strait.

On 8 February, the Japanese began an intense artillery barrage on the Australian sector in Singapore's North West. The artillery fire was very accurate and continued over the course of the day. The Commander of the 18th Battalion, Lieutenant-Colonel A. L Varley stated that he had never experienced a heavier bombardment, and this was a man who had served on several fronts during the First World War.

On the night of 8 February, the Japanese commenced their invasion. They landed in the Western section across the strait as had been predicted by the Allied Commanders following the days heavy bombardment. The Australian 20th Battalion were the first defenders to encounter them as well as gunners of the Australian 4th Machine Gun Battalion. These gunners inflicted heavy casualties on the initial barges ferrying Japanese soldiers across, however, they had much less of an impact on the second wave of armoured landing craft. The invasion vessels continued to come across the Strait from all directions all along the north-west coast. The Australians continued firing throughout the night at any shapes that appeared on the water, however, Yamashita's two best divisions, the 5th and the 18th, got about 13,000 men across that night and a further 10,000 the following dawn. The small Australian force of about 1,000 inflicted substantial casualties on the Japanese but were unable to halt the relentless surge of boats and men.

The ferocious defence of the Australians had taken a heavy toll on them as well, with 334 killed and a further 214 wounded. As would be expected, the forward battalions who had borne the brunt of the Japanese invasion, came out the worst. One company of 145 soldiers who had been right at the front had 57 killed, 22 wounded and another 66 taken prisoner, who, given the Japanese propensity for not taking prisoners were most likely taken to the rear and bayoneted to death.

By 11 February, the defenders had been forced back into a small perimeter around Singapore City and the Japanese had occupied the village and hill of Bukit Timah with its considerable food and oil supplies.

Winston Churchill sent a cable to Wavell that night saying:

'I think you ought to realise the way we view the situation in Singapore. It was reported to Cabinet by the Chief of the Imperial General Staff, General Alan Brooke, that Percival has over 100,000 men, of whom 33,000 are British and 17,000 Australian. It is doubtful whether the Japanese have as many in the entire Malay Peninsula. In these circumstances the defenders must greatly outnumber Japanese forces who have crossed the straits, and in a well contested battle they should destroy them. There must at this stage be no thought of saving the troops or sparing the population. The battle must be fought to the bitter end at all costs. Commanders and senior officers should die with their troops. The honour of the British Empire and of the British Army is at stake. I rely on you to show no mercy or weakness in any form. With the Russians fighting as they are and the Americans so stubborn at Luzon, the whole reputation of our country and our race is involved. It is expected that every unit will be brought in to close contact with the enemy and fight it out'.

Wavell was not ruthless enough to send out a directive of this nature, and issued his own order stating: 'in some units the troops have not shown the fighting spirit which is to be expected of men of the British Empire – the spirit of aggression and determination to stick it out must be inculcated in all ranks. There must be no more withdrawal without orders'.

These words did nothing to boost morale, particularly as they came from a commander who was not even present at the battle. On 13 February, Percival held a conference of his generals, including Gordon Bennett, the commander of the Australian forces, where it was agreed that further resistance was hopeless. Ammunition was rapidly disappearing and morale among the soldiers was collapsing. The Generals knew that the Japanese would take the fight right into the town of Singapore itself, which would cause massive civilian casualties. Thousands had already been killed by the relentless bombing and artillery fire and the civilians had nowhere to run to. The Generals agreed to contact Wavell and ask for permission to surrender.

By 15 February Singapore was on the verge of collapse. Japanese planes and artillery commenced their bombardment of the city at first light. Early that afternoon, Percival realised that the Battle for Singapore was as good as over. Japanese planes had free reign over the city and in the absence of military targets had bombed a hospital as well as St Andrews Cathedral. A deputation approached the Japanese front along Bukit Timah road requesting permission to surrender. Yamashita responded that Percival himself would have to make the surrender as such was his contempt for the Colonial rulers of Asia that he refused to accept the surrender from an inferior officer. Forcing the top British Commander to parade in front of Japanese journalists and cameramen, with the British flag in hand at Yamashita's order, would ensure maximum humiliation for the British Empire and, in Yamashita's mind, the transfer of power from one empire to another. By the end of 15 February, Japan had taken control of Singapore and added this jewel in the crown to its impressive list of territorial acquisitions since 7 December 1941, Hong Kong, New Britain and Malaya. They occupied Manchuria, as well as about 30 percent of China. Korea, Vietnam (French Indochina) and Thailand had also fallen to them. Their plans for 1942 involved controlling Indonesia (The Dutch East Indies), the Philippines, Burma and New Guinea. Australia was now firmly in their sights. And as demonstrated by the bravery, tenacity, endurance and discipline of Yamashita's fine soldiers, Australia had good reason to be extremely worried.

In the early stages of the Singapore
campaign, confidence remained high.

The Japanese victory at Singapore was swift and decisive.

Surrender at Singapore.

FACING A JAPANESE ASSAULT

For the young Australian soldiers based in Singapore, who were sweltering in the tropical heat and being physically drained from the constant hacking through thick rain forest, facing the Japanese along the defensive front that was constantly moving was a nerve-wracking experience.

The tactics of the Japanese were ruthless, as well as being very costly. Their commanders would send continual waves of attackers on to the Australian positions in an effort to determine the exact location of their guns. When the Australians unleashed fire in return on to the marauding attackers, cutting them to pieces, the Japanese artillery and mortars would zero in on their positions and commence firing. As the machine gun and rifle bullets whizzed past and the artillery fire fell, the jungle foliage very quickly thinned out as the leaves fell and trees were uprooted, turning the previously dense jungle into a killing field of fire that became clearer by the minute.

The Australians were only about 50 yards from the front line Japanese infantry men; however, they could not see them as they were camouflaged in the jungle. When a Japanese attack was about to commence, the Australian soldier's spines tingled in nervous fear as they could hear the preparations on the Japanese side. Firstly, from about 200 yards away, at the rear of the Japanese positions, a guttural, shouted order could be heard by the Australians, which was the precursor to the launch of the attack. Closer then to their positions, they could hear the mumbling from the Japanese lines as the order was quickly passed down the chain of command, and then, this was succeeded by noisy chatter and gibberish all the way along the front line, as if the men in the leading sections were assuring each other that they were all starting out together at the same time. As the chatter ceased, they would rush from their concealment, leaping towards the Australian positions in a coordinated line.

In larger attacks, those involving say two or more companies, a system of chanting the orders from the rear to the front was used, probably to ensure a simultaneous assault by all the Japanese sections charging from the forest together in unison as they could not see each other. Away in the distance, a powerful Japanese voice would chant a few words. Somewhere closer to the front line three or four more voices would merge together to repeat the phrase, and then, at the front itself, a dozen or so junior commanders would take up the refrain in unison. At this point, right along the front line, the final, urgent order would rise from the soldiers as they rushed forward to attack the Australian positions.

If the attacking Japanese received heavy losses from the defenders' mortars, machine guns and concentrated rifle fire, and it became clear that to press on with the attack would only result in further heavy casualties, this news somehow filtered back through the forest to the rear of the Japanese positions. From the darkness of the jungle, a shrill and clear bugle call would ring out, and on hearing this, the attackers would turn and vanish back into the jungle as quickly as they had come from it. The surviving Australians then faced an eerie quietness broken only by the calls from the wounded, as they nervously lit cigarettes with their shaking hands and looked around to see who was still alive.

If the attack was successful, as was most often the case in the Singapore Campaign, the Japanese soldiers would then occupy the Australian positions and regroup. Wounded soldiers would be dispatched, and any that surrendered were generally bayoneted or shot by the victorious troops who, still flushed with the heat of battle, had no time for prisoners as they quickly prepared for their next orders and tried to clean weapons, then reequip themselves with ammunition for the next stage of the attack.

Preparing to defend against a Japanese assault.

JAPANESE INVASION
PLANS FOR AUSTRALIA

Following his success at Singapore, General Yamashita, also known as the 'Tiger of Malaya', commenced his urgings to his commanders that the Imperial War machine continue onwards to occupy Australia. The Japanese High Command had not given much thought to Australia, largely because by merely looking at a map, it seemed too far away and represented nothing but a major supply problem if invaded. However, Yamashita saw otherwise. He realised that with the fall of the US forces in the Philippines, the Allies would need a base from which to mount an attack to retake them and ultimately engage Japan itself and Australia would be that perfect base. If Japan was able to occupy Australia, the problems of supply over the vast distances would rest with the Allies, and not with the Japanese.

Yamashita's success at Singapore had in no small way greatly enhanced his standing and his prestige skyrocketed. Prime Minister Tojo's ambition was to take Burma and then

India, the jewel in the British Empire's crown, in his bid to destroy the Empire, but Yamashita wrote to him urging him to garrison Malaya and Burma and attack Australia: 'Singapore, the great British bastion in the Far East, has fallen into our hands. The Allies are effectively sealed off'.

Although the Japanese Army and Navy were in constant conflict with each other over their own superiority and influence, Yamashita and Admiral Yamamoto had reasonably good relations. Yamashita used this relationship to get Yamamoto to help him lobby Prime Minister Tojo to give the order for the invasions. Yamamoto's carrier fleet would provide the aircraft to bomb the Australian cities and after smashing them, provide the transports to land his troops.

Yamashita's plan for the invasion of Australia was certainly bold, however, given his routing of Allied forces at Singapore with a much smaller force, his optimism could surely be understood. His plan was to conduct a number of small dummy landings at various locations in northern Queensland. The purpose of these landings would be to confuse the Australians and force them to send the best of their remaining forces to combat them. This would effectively leave the east coast and the centre of Australia largely undefended.

He then planned to land a division at Darwin after it had been pulverised by planes from the carriers provided by Yamamoto and he would land another division north of Brisbane. Following the fall of Darwin, his force of around 30,000 would travel by rail and road to Larrimah, about 300 kilometres south of Katherine. After decamping there for only a short period of time, they would complete the next, formidable, part of their journey and travel by dirt track about 1,000 kilometres to Alice Springs. This would require considerable transportation, but Yamashita was of the view that the men could again complete this journey on bicycle. He reasoned that they had travelled some 900 kilometres on rough terrain through Thailand and Malaya by bicycle, so it could be done again in Australia's desert. He would insist on the air force providing protection at all times.

The town of Alice Springs would be turned into one of the Japanese Army and Air Force's main bases. From here, and using a combination of bicycles, road transportation and trains, they would continue to Adelaide via convoluted stops in the towns of Maree, Quorn and Terowie. The reason for the long stops would be to allow the reversing and direction changing of trains, and to allow for the change from narrow gauge to broad gauge rail lines. Once Adelaide was occupied Yamashita planned to move the divisions to Melbourne, a distance of 800 kilometres.

Whilst this was all happening, the other Japanese division would capture Brisbane and then advance down to Sydney. Each city would be enveloped by a huge pincer movement that would effectively see them isolated. Any chance of help from the sea was out of the question given the huge resources and massive battleships and battle cruisers of the Japanese navy that would be patrolling up and down the coast in support of the military operation. In addition, the loss of the *Prince of Wales* and *Repulse* had rendered the British navy in the area non-existent, and a large portion of the American Pacific battle fleet was damaged or destroyed in Pearl Harbour.

Without troops to defend Sydney or Brisbane, as the best Australian divisions were either in the Middle East, or recently captured in Singapore, these cities would fall in much the same way as Singapore itself fell. Should the local population decide to resist, Yamashita would have no hesitation in ordering the air force to pulverise them, targeting civilians in the process. He was virtually prepared to do anything, including ordering the maximum destruction of innocent targets to get Australia to capitulate as quickly as possible.

There was a fair degree of conjecture between the Japanese commanders as to just how many soldiers would be needed for the invasion. In December, Admiral Inoue and Admiral Konda, who were broadly supportive of Yamashita felt they needed three divisions. Yamashita, who was acutely aware of, and considerably worried about his supply lines suggested that two divisions would be suitable for the two-pronged invasion. Yamamoto, who had far less concerns about supply lines, but had a much greater reputation for prudency and thinking through of military situations, felt that in view of the vastness of Australia and distances that the invading forces would need to travel, five divisions would be needed.

Even Yamamoto's estimate, which was more than double the estimate of Yamashita, was far below the estimates of the Australian, and Allied Commanders. They were of the view that anywhere between six and 12 divisions would be required to subjugate Australia, depending largely on the strategy decided on by the Japanese for their invasion. Yamashita's estimate of only two divisions was anything but ill-considered though. It must be remembered that this was double the number of men he had had under his command to take Malaya and Singapore, and the battle of Singapore was against much more experienced British and Australian troops (including the Australian 8th division) than were left now to defend Australia and his experienced, brave and highly motivated soldiers. Yamashita was of the belief that he would be fighting against perhaps only a quarter of the troops he had faced off against in Singapore.

Yamashita had certainly thought through his plan very well, and his main argument was a good one. This was that the Australian army simply did not have enough troops to organise a defence against the Japanese army, and this is completely forgetting the argument over the differing fighting qualities of the potential opposing forces. He stated, 'All they could ever hope to do was to make a guerrilla resistance in the bush'. Once he had taken control of Brisbane and Sydney, he did not see any difficulty in subduing Australia. 'It would never be my intention to take over the entire country. It was too large', he remarked. 'With its coastline, anyone can always land there exactly when he wants'. Given the size and strength of the Japanese navy at this stage of the war and the size of its ships that would roam the coastline it is hard to disagree.

Yamashita also believed that once he was in control of Australia it would be relatively simple to defend it. The main reason for this was based on the same reasons that Prime Minister Tojo was reluctant to even consider an invasion of Australia. The issue was supply. Tojo felt that the distance of Australia from Japan and its bases would make the supply of its invading force nigh on impossible. Yamashita believed that for the same reason once he had captured it, it would be too far for the Allied supply lines to attempt to recapture it. This is a very relevant argument given that the Allies had a multitude of other areas to attempt to recapture and defend following the success of the Japanese campaign through the Pacific. Yamashita was not afraid to boast to anyone that questioned his plan that his two divisions of occupying troops would be more than sufficient to repel any Anglo-American 'invasions' of his newly conquered Australian territory.

He was dismissive of Tojo's concern about the over-stretched supply lines. The huge country was such a vulnerable target that once he had marched his army in and defeated it, the long supply lines would be a bigger problem for the British and Americans. In fact, so convinced was he of this view that Yamashita felt that when all the fighting for Australia was over, and the Allies had sat down to consider the supply line problem, they would most likely abandon Australia all together and focus their efforts against other, more realistic targets.

Tojo found himself forced to consider these plans for the invasion of Australia, particularly given the reverence in which Yamashita and Yamamoto were being held in by the Japanese emperor and the media. The main reason for this is that if he did not, he faced the real prospect that Australia could become the main US base in the Pacific to begin a counter attack. Admiral Yamamoto was strongly of the belief that the Port of Darwin, in Australia's north, would potentially grow into the Americans most useful, and functional, military base and needed to be put out of action. To do this, he proposed using the same carrier force that he had sent to wreak havoc at Pearl Harbor only two months prior. The attack would be led by the same pilot who had successfully led the attacks against the US Pacific fleet,

Captain Mitsuo Fuchida. His planes would take off from the same aircraft carriers, using the same air crews.

There would be a difference though. The bombing of Darwin would be far more severe than the bombing of Pearl Harbor. The Japanese felt in hindsight that they had been mistaken at Pearl Harbor by not sending enough planes in the first wave and for not wreaking a greater amount of damage than they did. Darwin had far more target ships than Pearl Harbor for a start. In addition, this time they would change their strategy for this attack. The first wave of carrier-based planes would target the airfields, ships in the harbour and generally operate in the same manner as the attack on Pearl. The second wave, however, would not comprise carrier-based aircraft, but larger bombers launched from air bases on land. These larger bombers would be bigger, and capable of carrying much heavier pay loads. They would target the port and airfields as well, but they would also seek with their destructive power to destroy the city. The Japanese were far less concerned with the potential Australian reaction to the deaths of civilians that might occur. Destroying Darwin would prove to the leader-ship of Japan that Australia could be taken without fuss. It would also enable Yamamoto and Yamashita to continue to push on with their demands for their invasion plans. In the meantime, Yamamoto, and the rest of the Japanese admirals were looking forward to their opportunity for their next big carrier-based bombing raid after Pearl Harbor.

General Tomoyuki Yamashita (The Tiger of Malaya)

THE BOMBING OF DARWIN

This next big bombing raid took place less than three months after the attack at Pearl Harbour against the Port of Darwin in northern Australia. Four Japanese aircraft carriers – *Akagi, Kaga, Hiryù* and *Sòryù* – positioned themselves 350 kilometres northwest of Darwin. They were escorted by the battleships *Hei* and *Kirishima*; two heavy cruisers, *Tone* and *Chikuma*, the light cruiser *Abukuma*, and nine destroyers. In fact, this was the very same armada that was used to attack Pearl Harbour, although with two fewer aircraft carriers. As formidable as this fleet was, it would not itself be engaged in the attack, the entire assault would come from the air. As dawn broke on Thursday 19 February 1942, the carriers were arming their aircraft and warming their engines. The growl of this mass of engines could be heard up to 100 kilometres away, accentuated by the shrill sound of the vicious little Zero fighters darting across the early morning sky.

Vice Admiral Nagumo launched the first attack wave at 0845 hours in perfect weather, which was led by Captain

Fuchida. It comprised 71 dive bombers, 81 torpedo bombers and 36 Zero fighters. Their target was to be all of Darwin's major installations, its oil storage tanks, and the 46 ships anchored in its harbour.

At 0915 hours, the Japanese force was first spotted by the communications station at HMAS Coonawarra, about nine kilometres west of Darwin; however, the report for some reason was not passed on to the appropriate commander. This meant that Darwin would not be aware of Fuchida's attack until his planes struck. The planes crossed the Northern Territory coast near Koolpinyah, east of Darwin and then turned north west and flew over Noonamah. The force of 188 fighters and bombers arrived at Darwin at 0958 hours, two minutes ahead of schedule. Five US Kittyhawk planes, which were returning from an aborted mission over Timor, ran into the Japanese air armada, but they were quickly dispatched by the highly efficient Zero fighters for which they were no match. The 81 torpedo bombers immediately headed towards the 46 ships in the harbour, whilst the dive bombers, closely escorted by the zeros, turned their attention to the RAAF bases, civil airfields as well as two hospitals. Crews at these bases scrambled to be airborne but they were caught unaware and their planes were destroyed before they could take off. Nine Australian and 11 American aircraft were destroyed.

The Japanese commander of the Air fleet, Captain Fuchida reported later:

'the job of flattening Darwin seemed hardly worthy of Nagumo force. The harbour, it is true, was crowded with all kinds of ships. But a single pier, and a few waterside buildings appeared to be the only port installations. The airfield on the outskirts of town, though fairly large, had no more than two or three small hangars. In all, there were only about 20-odd planes of various types scattered about the fields. No planes were in the air. A few attempted to take off as we came over but were quickly shot down, and the rest were destroyed where they stood. Anti-aircraft fire was intense but largely ineffectual, and we quickly accomplished our objectives'.

A second wave appeared eighty minutes later, this time including high altitude bombers with much greater payloads and these targeted the RAAF base at Parap. So orderly and disciplined were these attackers, that observers below likened it to an air display. Twenty-seven bombers approached from the south west and 27 from the north-east and as the two formations intercepted each other, formed a perfect V and then manoeuvred over the airstrip dropping 13 tonnes of bombs in their initial pass. The accuracy was perfect and as well as obliterating the runway, the force of the blast destroyed buildings and virtually disintegrated any planes that had been left damaged by the first attack wave.

The destruction of Darwin was clinical. The objectives of the Japanese were to make Darwin inoperable and irreparable. The destruction of the airfield at Parap was completed with such precision and force similar to the way the American fleet at Pearl Harbour had been treated, and the demolition of Singapore only days before. The Japanese were sending a clear message to Australia, if you chose to fight us and not submit to us, we will kill all of you, whether military or civilian.

According to official records, 243 people were killed at Darwin with more than 300 injured, but on the ground, witnesses tell a much different story. Padre Richards, a priest in the town scoffed at the official death toll. 'Two hundred and forty-three?' he asked, 'I buried more than that myself'. His view was that the rumoured figure of 1,100 issued by Army intelligence was far more accurate. The remains of the dead, which had decomposed terribly in the tropical heat of Darwin, were allegedly buried in mass graves at Mindil Beach.

The soldiers and police who were tasked with this horrible job all agreed that the death toll was well over a thousand people, four or five times the official number. The torpedo bombers operating against the ships in Darwin harbour sank eight of them, a combination of Australian, American and British. The biggest loss of life occurred aboard the USS *Peary*, 91 sailors aboard her lost their lives.

Following the attack on Darwin, about half of the population (around 2,500 people) fled the town. They could not believe that following such a ferocious attack on the city that an invasion could not be about to take place. Those that fled headed for the Adelaide River where a train was preparing to leave for the interior. This was sarcastically referred to by those that stayed behind in Darwin as the 'Adelaide River Stakes', and 278 servicemen based at RAAF Parap also deserted, attempting to flee the expected Japanese onslaught.

So chaotic was the rush that as the authorities inspected the town shortly after the exodus they observed just how disorderly it all was. Darwin's administrator Charles Lowe noted 'houses were abandoned in haste, letters started but not finished, papers strewn about, beds unmade...' A large amount of looting occurred but it was mostly to obtain food for the journey out of the town, although a lot of looting would go on for weeks. In fact, after much of the population had fled, military vehicles backed up to shops and loaded up with goods, and gangs of soldiers helped themselves to whatever they wanted such as clothes, ovens and refrigerators, even toys and pianos.

Prime Minister Curtin kept the nation uninformed as to the extent of the damage in Darwin, and the government was very concerned. If what happened in Darwin after the effect of a bombing raid could be a foretaste of what would happen elsewhere in Australia if the country was left disorganised, badly defended, without leadership and poorly equipped, the outcome could be disastrous. It would have absolutely no chance against an enemy that was highly motivated, professional, ruthless and operating a war machine which was rapidly becoming accustomed to easy victories in the air, on the sea and on the land, against every country it attacked and the armies, navies and air forces of any country which it put itself up against.

THE JAPANESE ZERO AND ITS PILOTS

The Japanese fighters had virtually not evolved over the course of the war, meaning that although in the initial stages of World War II, the Zero was a formidable weapon, by 1945 it was a shadow of its former self against the P-51 Mustangs and the US carrier-based fighters such as the Hellcats and the Corsairs.

In fact, such a formidable weapon was it in the early stages of the war that, when the pilots of the United States and England were up against it, the Zeros had almost complete control of the skies. In Malaya, as the Japanese Imperial forces swept forward, these fighter planes inflicted one lopsided victory after another. A pitched air battle erupted in the skies above Kota Bahru on the Malayan northeast coast when the Japanese put an invasion force ashore on the first day of the war. In as little as 20 minutes, the Japanese Zeros had shot down several Royal Air Force Bristol Blenheims, as well as several Lockheed Hudson bombers. To add insult to injury, a large number of Japanese G3M bombers appeared in the skies above which had been swept clear by their fighters and dropped bombs on the RAF runways and air base instal-lations, causing enormous damage. These bombers had flown from bases more than 600 miles away in Indochina. This air raid came as a massive surprise for the British, as they believed that the Japanese could never be capable of mounting an air strike over such a large distance.

The British air defences in Malaya had placed far too much reliance in the Brewster Buffalo, an unusual looking, and obsolete fighter purchased from the United States.

Pilots utterly despised the aircraft, with one saying it looked 'like the racing planes of the 1930s, all engine, a barrel fuselage, stubby wings, a large canopy, and almost no tail'. On top of this, the Buffalo was underpowered, it suffered fuel delivery problems that curtailed its rate of climb, and due to flawed landing gear, it was prone to serious damage on landing, that often also caused serious injury, if not death to pilots. It mounted .50 calibre guns, however, these were prone to jamming, particularly in the humidity of the tropics. The Buffalo proved to be no match against the speed and the dexterity of the Zeros.

In Malaya, as in the Philippines, the Allied air forces were not prepared for the sudden onslaught which they encountered from the Japanese and this multiplied their non-combat losses. Many British and American aircraft crashed due to engine failures, accidents or mid-air collisions with other aircraft. Planes were being shot down by friendly anti-aircraft fire whilst returning to their bases which reflected the edginess of the gunners in the anti-aircraft batteries, and their lack of experience, training and battle conditioning. Many planes were forced to ditch due to a lack of fuel, others managed to land safely but had to be scrapped nonetheless due to damage incurred on landing. From the Japanese perspective a crashed plane was every bit as good as one shot down – in some respects even better as it required no expenditure of ammunition on their part. If the aircrew went down with it, then even better still.

A great deal of arrogance towards their enemy was held by the British and American pilots and stemmed from a widely held conviction developed over the years before the war that Japanese airpower was not to be viewed seriously. This idea was promoted by a number of so called 'experts' of various fields, with their theories. The Japanese could never make decent pilots, according to the military authorities because of the physiological defects they suffered by comparison to their Western counterparts. They were cross eyed and near sighted, possibly a symptom of their 'slanted' eyes. Japanese mothers carried their infants on their backs, causing their heads to wobble and therefore throwing off the balance in their inner ear. Japanese cultural behaviour maintained obedience and conformity. As a result, young men would not carry the traits of daring, individualism and self-reliance, so important in an aviator, particularly a fighter pilot. Western air force military journals cited numerous 'statistics' that Japan had the highest aviation crash rate in the world. The Allies did acknowledge that the Japanese had developed their own self–sufficient aircraft manufacturing industry, admittedly a surprising achieve-ment, but the general idea that planes built in Japan by the likes of Mitsubishi, Kawasaki and Nakajima could be any good was simply not worth a moments consideration.

It was not really until after the huge losses of late 1941 that the Allies began to realise that they had only seen what the Japanese wanted them to see. As Sun Tzu had written, 'if he (your enemy) is arrogant, behave timidly to encourage his arrogance'.

The reality was that the Japanese naval pilots were among the very best pilots in the world. The selection process involved a highly competitive recruiting program and to earn their wings, they had to survive long and intense training regimens. On average they were far more accomplished than their British and American opposite numbers. A number of their pilots had flown over 100 missions already in China, amassing an average of 500 hours in the cockpit. They were profoundly motivated and disciplined and eager to correct the misconception that the West had developed about them. They showed resourcefulness, adaptability and endurance, they worked very well in a team, and they would exploit any weakness shown by their opposition with ruthlessness.

The Mitsubishi A6M Zero was a champion in a dogfight, an acrobatic plane that out-turned, out-climbed, and out-manoeuvred any of the fighter planes that the Allies could put up against it. In terms of its armaments, it packed two 7.7 mm machine guns which were synchronised to fire between the propeller blades, as well as two highly powerful wing-mounted 20 mm cannons. It delighted in low-speed, low-altitude 'tail chasing' which, due to its tight turning circle, allowed it to get behind any Allied plane and quickly destroy it with a short accurate burst. Dismayed Allied pilots even spoke of it flipping over on its back and appearing behind them before they even knew what was going on. The Japanese aviators loved the planes responsiveness to their touch on the controls and the fact that the aircraft would respond with only the slightest pressure on the joystick. Fighter pilot Saburo Sakai said, 'She handled like a dream', adding 'just a flick of my wrist and she was gone! I went through all sorts of aerobatics, standing the Zero on her tail, diving, sliding off the wings'. Allied pilots fought the Zeros using traditional dogfighting techniques which involved chasing and manoeuvring to get on the enemy's tail, but the Zeros shot them down in vast numbers. The ones that did escape from these lethal fighters, by either escaping into a cloud in the sky, or parachuting to the ground from their own bullet riddled plane were in awe of this newly discovered fighter and the men that flew them.

The Zero came into service for the Japanese navy and air force in the summer of 1940, about a year and a half before Pearl Harbour. Over the course of the war 11,000 of the machines were built. The Zeros had accompanied Japanese bombers on long range missions into China, operating from their bases on Formosa and elsewhere along the Chinese coast. By the specifications of that time, the range the aircraft was capable of flying was quite extraordinary. By managing fuel mixtures and adjusting propeller speeds, it was demonstrated that it was possible to fly this single seat plane over 1,000 miles (1,600 kilometres) on a single tank of petrol. So reliable was the operation of the plane, that pilots who were exhausted at the end of such a long mission, would even set the trim to level flight and doze in the cockpit on the flight home. So effective was the Zero against Chiang Kai-Shek's Chinese national air force, that in 1940 and 1941 following its arrival into service, not a single Zero was downed in air to air combat over China.

One American, General Claire Lee Chennault, who commanded the 'Flying Tigers', an American group of volunteers who fought alongside the Chinese Air Force, had come into contact with these Japanese fighters before Pearl Harbour. They flew the Curtis P-40 Warhawk, a single engine, single seated fighter which was also the backbone of American air defences at Pearl Harbour. General Chennault coached the P-40 pilots on how to fight the Zero, dive from altitude, stay close to your wingman, set up passing shots, and 'never try to dogfight a Zero, particularly in turning combat. Hit and run! Hit and run, dive and then come back to altitude. Always try and stay in groups of at least two. As soon as you find yourself alone, search the skies to rejoin someone'. Chennault provided several intelligence reports to Washington; however, the defence brass chose to ignore them. The Americans simply could not believe that the Japanese were capable of designing, building and manufacturing an aircraft with a climb rate of 3,000 feet per minute. So, for a year and a half, although in full operation in China and even coming into contact with American pilots such as those commanded by Chennault, the Zero remained an almost complete unknown in Allied aviation circles. It was not until Pearl Harbour and the subsequent Japanese invasions to the south, that the plane became known to the British and American pilots in the most lethal way. It was another example of the arrogance of the West, even though receiving plentiful evidence of the various threats from Japan. This was an arrogance unfortunately that would ultimately cause the deaths of hundreds of aircrews and the destruction of hundreds of planes in the initial months of the war in the Pacific.

The Japanese Zero was a very formidable
aircraft in the early stages of the war.

JAPANESE OCCUPATION
INTENTIONS

The Japanese plans for the occupation of Australia, with such a small number of troops when considering the vastness of the country was quite simple – apply a level of ruthlessness of an unimaginable scale and apply it equally towards both enemy combatants and innocent civilians to terrify the population against even attempting any form of resistance.

It has already been mentioned that Yamashita's plans for any resistance by local populations would be met by a show of power from Japan's air force to destroy any points of resistance no matter where they might be and to make no effort to limit civilian casualties in the process. In fact, his view was that the more civilian casualties that occurred the more likely the Australians would be to cease any resistance whatsoever.

Australians who may have had any lingering doubt as to how ruthless the Japanese occupiers might be, need only look at a couple of very recent instances to quickly dispel these doubts.

On 12 February 1942, and with the fall of Singapore imminent, 64 Australian nurses were evacuated from the city on a small steamship *Vyner Brook*. On board with the nurses were over 200 civilians and English military personnel. Between Sumatra and Borneo, the ship was strafed and bombed by Japanese aircraft and quickly sank.

The survivors who made it into lifeboats were strafed again by the Japanese planes but some of them managed to reach Bangka Island off the Sumatran coast. Twelve Australian nurses were either killed in the attack on the ship or drowned in the ocean, but 53 did reach Bangka Island by lifeboat, raft or drifting with the tide.

The nurses had their red cross armbands which offered them protective status as non-combatants under the Geneva convention. As such, the nurses expected to be treated in a civilised manner by their Japanese captors. These hopes were unfortunately short lived. About 30 who had splintered into a group that landed at a part of the island were herded into a filthy and overcrowded building by the Japanese at gunpoint. They were tired, hungry, thirsty and some were suffering horrifying levels of sunburn which they had incurred after many hours immersed in the sea. In addition, some of them were wounded from the strafing attacks both on the ship and the lifeboats. The Japanese were unsympathetic to them and offered them only a bucket of water and a bucket of rice.

On 16 February another group of 22 nurses found their way to a separate section of Bangka island with around 100 other refugees, including many children. Whilst there they started attending to the sailors and soldiers in the group who were injured. They had no food or water or medical supplies, so it was decided that in the best interests of all they would surrender to the Japanese.

An officer from the *Vyner Brooke* went to find the Japanese in the village of Muntok on the north-west of the Island to surrender to them. While he was away, Matron Irene Drummond suggested that the civilian women and children walk towards Muntok whilst the nurses cared for the men. At mid-morning the ships officer returned with about twenty Japanese soldiers. The soldiers separated the men and the women prisoners, then divided the men into two groups and marched them along the beach and behind a headland. The nurses heard a quick succession of shots and then the Japanese soldiers returned, sat in front of them and began cleaning their rifles and bayonets.

A Japanese officer arrived and ordered the nurses to leave the shelter of the palm trees and walk into the water until they were waist deep. A couple of soldiers shoved those who were slow to respond. As the women stood in a line in the water, some of the soldiers brought a machine gun down to the beach. Matron Irene Drummond called out 'chins up girls, I'm proud of you and I love you all'. At that point the machine gun began firing up and down the line of women and the girls fell one after the other. Only one survived, nurse Vivian Bullwinkel, who had been hit in the back by a bullet and thrown forward into the ocean. Upon discovering that she was only wounded, she pretended to be dead. After some time had passed she risked a look back at the beach and saw that the Japanese soldiers had gone. She looked around for her 21 comrades but saw no-one.

When she reached the beach, she was joined by an English soldier who had survived the massacre behind the headland. Private Cecil Kingsley had been bayoneted and left for dead. They managed to reach a village but were given only a small amount of food by the local village women, as the men of the village forbade helping them. They were worried that if Bullwinkel and Kingsley were found by the Japanese and it could be seen that the villagers had rendered assistance, there would be repercussions for the village. Bullwinkel spent the next twelve days with Kingsley, tending to his severe wounds as well as her own. The Japanese bullet had passed completely through her body but fortunately had missed her vital organs. Realising that their position was hopeless they decided to give themselves up and set off toward Muntok. Shortly after, Kingsley died from his bayonet wounds and Bullwinkel was taken into captivity by the Japanese. Bullwinkel realised that all the survivors of the *Vyner Brooke* would be at risk if the Japanese discovered what she had seen so she concealed her wound from the Japanese and continued to treat it herself. Her imprisonment was harsh; however, she managed to survive, and went on to give evidence of the massacre at a war crimes tribunal in Tokyo in 1947.

In another incident, some battalions of Australia's 8th division were retreating through Malaya with the sole purpose of making it to Singapore without being captured by the Japanese army who was hot on their heels. They were attempting to withdraw, by night, to a village named Parit Surlong, about 130 kilometres from Johore Bahru and the Singapore causeway. Casualties were mounting whilst fighting desperate rear-guard actions so before long, within their number were many wounded soldiers. This caused the convoy to become filled with trucks and ambulances transporting these wounded. Their leader, the bespectacled Lieutenant-Colonel Charles Anderson had ordered his medical officers not to leave any wounded in the 'hot' battle areas. It was widely known that the Japanese showed no mercy towards prisoners, particularly wounded ones who were regarded as liabilities and were executed.

Ammunition was extremely low and Anderson had ordered his forces, comprising the $2/19^{th}$ and $2/29^{th}$ battalions of Australians and the Indian 45th brigade, to make fixed bayonet charges. After 18 hours of withdrawal, and many forced battles along the way, he arrived with his depleted force at the outskirts of Parit Surlong.

Anderson then considered his options and realised that he needed to push on to brigade headquarters on the coast at Yong Peng, around 60 kilometres away. This would require an assault on the main town of Parit Surlong to overwhelm the Japanese defending it and to then continue forward. The Japanese had set up machine gun defences and light artillery to defend the main bridge through the town. In addition, the Australians had received some tinned food, morphine and medical supplies by air drop the previous day but had not received any ammunition. The lack of ammunition meant that Anderson had to make a decision on how to reach Yong Peng with the Japanese crack troops barring his way.

He realised that his only alternative was to go through the jungle but that would mean that many of his wounded would be unable to go. In fact, only the wounded who could walk, or walk with the assistance of another man, would be capable of attempting the jungle breakthrough with the main force. He attempted to liaise with the Japanese in the hope that they would let the wounded men in the truck and ambulance convoy cross the bridge and travel on to Yong Peng. The Japanese refused outright.

This refusal meant that Anderson had to leave the most incapacitated men behind. This numbered 110 Australian diggers and 35 Indian soldiers, as well as 10 only slightly wounded men, who, in an act of great bravery, volunteered to stay behind and tend to their badly injured comrades, even though they knew that this decision meant that they would soon be taken prisoner by the Japanese. Anderson then gave the order for his fit men, and the wounded who could be assisted, to move out into the jungle, avoiding the roads, to attempt to reach Yong Peng leaving the sick and wounded behind.

The following day the Japanese came over the bridge and surrounded the trucks and ambulances fearing that they might be booby-trapped. After discovering that they were full of wounded men they advanced with fixed bayonets and ordered them out. Those who were unable to move were dragged roughly from the vehicles and thrown to the ground where they remained for several hours.

The men were then placed into a farmhouse nearby and were left there for another night. The Japanese were unsure of what to do with these 155 prisoners that they had taken. The next morning, the Japanese General in charge of the Malaya campaign, General Yamashita came to the farmhouse raising the Australians hope of fair treatment. Yamashita was in a hurry and his urgency was the conquest of Singapore. After looking through the windows at the wounded men he ordered that there should be no delay to the push to the causeway separating Malaya and Singapore and that the wounded and their attendees should be disposed of.

After Yamashita left, the prisoners were put into groups of five, tied together with wire and dragged outside the farmhouse to a clearing. They were bayoneted, and machine gunned, until there was no movement. This continued in small groups of five for a couple of hours. At the end of the morning, the lifeless bodies were doused with petrol and they were set alight. Some of the Australian and Indian men who were only lightly bayoneted or had somehow survived their bullet wound had faked their own deaths. But as the flames engulfed their bodies, there was no faking their screams as they were slowly incinerated.

THE JAPANESE PAUSE
ON INVASION PLANS

U ltimately though, the Japanese came to the realisation that the invasion and occupation of Australia would be a huge commitment of resources to an already stretched military. The debate in Japan, over what to do about Australia, began to descend into a no holds barred argument. Prime Minister Tojo had been undecided even after the success of the operations in Malaya and Singapore, but as he came under more pressure from Yamashita and Yamamoto, the Imperial Forces most successful commanders from their respective branches he began to express his doubts. His main concern was that it would cause manpower problems, and he instructed his subordinates to prepare a case against an invasion of the country.

Tojo took the decision to send Yamashita to a garrison command in Manchuria, which was a huge humiliation for the man who had led his forces to one of Japan's greatest victories in Malaya and Singapore. On top of this, Tojo issued him with travel orders that prevented him from receiving a hero's welcome. He was disallowed an audience with the emperor and effectively was shut completely out of the decision-making process.

On 27 February 1942, at a joint operation meeting in Tokyo at Imperial Headquarters, representatives from the army made their case to dismiss any idea of a plan for the invasion of Australia. They asked how the navy could possibly contemplate invading a country which was effectively the same size as China and double the size of the territory which they occupied in China. They argued that the manpower requirements put forward in Yamashita's plan were woefully inadequate and that in fact 12 divisions would be needed if they were to successfully invade and control the vast continent. This number was very close to Winston Churchill's assessment of Japan's requirement to invade Australia.

The comparisons with China were really an excuse to get out of the operation. It ignored the fact that Australia was virtually undefended and very sparsely populated compared to the 500 million Chinese population. Although the Japanese army was clearly superior to the Chinese army, a population of that size, with the right leadership, had great capacity to organise guerrilla resistance, particularly in the remoter parts.

The army and navy continued to argue over the invasion, with the army's chief of operations, Colonel Takushoro Hattori, becoming increasingly angry with his counterpart in the navy, Baron Tomioka, who presented the very telling point, that 'the enemy (America) has to be denied the use of Australia as a base. As long as the enemy has no foothold there, Australia can be taken'. He had certainly done his research. Australia's sparseness was both a strength and a weakness. But one thing was undeniable. The nation was inadequately defended, and the Japanese forces were very powerful, and very good. They would have no regard for the civilian defences which would be put up to attempt to stop them and they would be tossed aside. Tomioka then stated, 'if within the next two years the United States concentrates rapidly on aircraft production and makes full use of Australia, Japan would never be able to resist the material onslaught which would follow'.

This was a very confronting prognosis, particularly at a point in time at which Japan seemed invincible and its Army, Navy and Air Force were effortlessly sweeping all before them. Hattori was livid with rage at this further point put to him by the eloquently spoken Tomioka. He picked up a cup of tea and holding it away from the table stated, 'the tea in this cup represents our total naval strength'. He then turned it over spilling the contents to the ground at which point he spat 'you see, it just goes so far!' He glared at Tomioka as he stood from the table and stated, 'if your plan is approved, I will resign'. He bowed, and he left the room with the army planners close behind.

Australia needed to be dealt with but now perhaps was not quite the time.

FORTRESS FREMANTLE

The Port of Fremantle, from where the *USS Bullhead* embarked on 31 July 1945 to commence her final, fateful mission, was in fact one of the biggest, and busiest, submarine bases of World War II. In fact, if there had been as few as twenty more patrols out of Fremantle, it would have been the busiest submarine base of the entire war. The busiest was Pearl Harbour, in the US state of Hawaii. Up to 170 American, Dutch and British submarines operated out of Fremantle during the war. As the Japanese began their daring and brutal advance south after severely damaging the American pacific fleet at Pearl Harbour, the submarines of these nations had raced to find a base that they could continue to operate out of. The American submarines came largely from the Philippines, which the Japanese attacked at the same time as Pearl Harbour and conquered in April 1942. The British submarines came primarily from Malaya and Singapore, which fell to the Japanese on 15 February 1942, shortly after the British battle fleet 'Force Z' was sunk off the coast of Malaya, and the Dutch submarines came from the Dutch East Indies, now Indonesia, which was invaded by the Japanese shortly before Singapore fell.

The defences of Fremantle though had been planned well before Australia stood to defend itself against Japan in early 1942. It was as early as 1933, that the Australian government put together a program to increase coastal defences around the country. Although Japan had been at war against China in Manchuria since 1931, it was never really regarded as a threat to Australia, largely due to its treaty obligations in place with Britain and the United States, which greatly reduced the size of its once mighty navy. At the Washington naval conference of 1921-22, the Japanese had agreed to cap the aggregate tonnage of its battleship fleet to 60 percent of the US and British totals. This treaty mirrored a consensus, born about after the First World War, that the great world powers must avoid another expensive naval arms race.

The reduction in Japans cap was rationalised by its lack of commitments elsewhere in the Pacific compared to the British and American navies. It was felt that Japan could maintain its entire fleet close to home while the American and British navies also had to concern themselves with the Atlantic. This 60 percent reduction, expressed as a 5:5:3 ratio was extended in 1930 to auxiliary ships as well by the London Naval Disarmament treaty. These treaty limitations at the time were largely supported by Emperor Hirohito and even most of the senior admirals of the navy as it meant that by imposing limits on battleship development, the down-sized battleship program would allow further emphasis on carrier development and other categories outside of the treaty provisions. Also, the treaty spared Japan the burden of entering into a naval arms race with the west when the industrial side of its economy was still emerging and fragile when compared to the might of the industrial capacity of the US and Britain. In 1921, naval spending absorbed over 30 percent of Japans budget. The treaty participation brought that figure down to about 20 percent by 1923. Japan was in fact on the verge of bankruptcy, therefore military disarmament in the 1920s would offer much needed fiscal relief. Japanese hard liners on the other hand cared little about the economic situation and bemoaned the reduction in size of the Japanese battleship fleet, and what they saw as pandering to the west that held Japan in scant regard, despite Japans recent military successes. These successes included the absorption of the Kurile Islands north of Hokkaido in 1875, the Bonin Islands south of Japan in 1876 and the Ryukyu Islands which included Okinawa in 1879. Japan fought a war against China in 1894-95 in which it was victorious, as well as defeating Russia in 1904-05. This included the naval battle of Tsushima, widely regarded as one of the greatest naval successes of all time, in which the Japanese navy encountered the Russian battle fleet that had sailed three quarters of the way around the world in the Tsushima Straight, and sent it to the bottom of the ocean in a matter of hours.

Despite all this, it was as a matter of fact Germany who set the alarm bells ringing in the Australian governments ears and triggered the coastal defence review. There was ill wind in Europe, and in March 1933, Adolf Hitler's National Socialist German Workers (Nazi) party was elected into office on the back of a campaign promising an expansion of the German empire, which began causing consternation not just in Europe but around the world.

Fremantle was recognised as a major port for defence not because of its future role as a submarine base, but because of its strategic location. It was already the second busiest harbour in Australia, after Sydney, and from a military perspective it would be of vital importance for supply as well as being an embarkation point for troops leaving the country to fight as it had been in World War 1.

As a result, its defences were extensive. The entire harbour was protected by gun emplacements and batteries that provided an enormous zone of fire that would, in theory, protect it from any invading naval force. In total there were no less than 11 gun batteries, each with varying levels of armament, to protect the port.

On Rottnest Island, which due to its location was often referred to as the gatekeeper of the Port of Fremantle, there was a battery at Oliver Hill which comprised two 9.2 inch BL Mk X guns. These huge guns, with a range of 28 kilometres, were to provide a counter bombardment role by preventing an enemy ship from sitting offshore and bombarding ships, submarines and port facilities in Fremantle Harbour itself. There was also a battery at Bickley (two 6 inch BL Mk XI guns). Next to Bickley, and away from the main holiday accommodation, was built the Kingstown Barracks, which served to house the garrison for both batteries. A new jetty was built nearby, and it was connected to Kingstown and Oliver Hill by a light railway. At a location known as Signal Ridge on Rottnest Island, close to the Oliver Hill Battery, was the Fortress Command post, Rottnest Fire Command, the Northern Fire Command and the Fremantle Fire Command.

The original plan for the defence of Fremantle did not actually incorporate Rottnest Island at all, primarily due to the difficulty that would be faced in transporting the infrastructure over to the island. The 9.2 inch gun battery that was located at Oliver Hill was intended to be installed at Buckland Hill in Mosman Park. It was realised, however, that this location would not have prevented the long-range bombing of Fremantle Harbour by cruisers with 8 inch guns. Planning then shifted to Rottnest Island, where its location off the coast would ensure that it could engage targets with its long-range guns well before they reached a position to fire on Fremantle Harbour.

On the mainland, and near to Fremantle, the port defences continued. At Swanbourne there was a battery of two 6 inch BL Mk VII guns and the Mainland Fire Command was also based here. These Swanbourne guns were some of the oldest and came from the Fort Forrest site that was built as the original defences of Fremantle Harbour in the North Port area when the inner harbour was opened back in 1897. The Fort Forrest site was needed for port development, so in 1936 arrangements were made to move the guns up to Swanbourne and in 1938 the guns were proofed and placed on their permanent mounts. The guns were removed after the war and the Swanbourne Battery site became the base for the Special Air Services Regiment (the SAS) now known as Campbell Barracks.

At Leighton, there was a battery of two 6 inch BL Mk VII guns. These also came from the oldest defences of Fremantle at Fort Arthur Head, which was established north of the Fremantle Roundhouse also at the time of the opening of the harbour. The guns had been placed there in 1909. Again, with the continued development of the port, the ability to use the guns of the Arthur Battery became restricted and so in 1942, construction started at Buckland Hill to house the Leighton Battery. Moving these guns to Leighton meant that they could be better co-ordinated with the ones at Swanbourne, and Bickley on Rottnest Island to provide good defensive cover of Gage Roads and the channels leading into Fremantle.

In late 1942, another battery known as the Harbour Battery was formed. This comprised two 75 mm guns, which were installed at North Mole along with two 12 pounder guns which were placed at South Mole. There was also a 6 pounder gun at either end of the harbour boom gate. These weapons were very antiquated, and so in August 1943, with the war still in full swing and the threat still considerable, these were replaced with two twin 6 pounder guns which have a much greater rate of fire. Making up the Harbour Battery were six 40mm Bofors guns which were to provide defence against low flying aircraft attempting either torpedo or strafing runs against ships or submarines in the harbour.

The Fremantle defences spread further south into Cockburn sound, primarily around Garden Island. In February 1942 after Singapore fell, the Royal Navy put a request to the Australian Government to use Cockburn Sound as a base for its Far Eastern Fleet. Given that most of the existing defences had been put in place prior to the commencement of war, and the time required to design and then construct the defences, an interim counter-bombardment capacity was needed. Garden Island became the principal location for most of these.

Challenger Battery was established in July 1943, which comprised two 155 mm mobile guns. This was located at

Entrance Point on the north-western tip of Garden Island. From here it could engage and prevent enemy ships from standing to the west of Garden Island and bombarding Cockburn sound. On the north-eastern tip was the Beacon Battery, which was made up of two 4 inch QF Mk IX naval guns which covered the area north from Garden Island down to Woodman Point. In 1938, following the installation of the heavy 9.2 inch guns located at Oliver Hill on Rottnest Island, a battery of these was proposed for Garden Island as well to supplement those on Rottnest Island; however, the proposal was postponed before construction commenced. This battery, known as Scriven, was recommenced in mid-1943 on the west coast of Garden Island. The construction of these took some time though, and although the guns were put in place, they were not fully operational until after the war.

To the south of Garden Island, the Peron Battery was established at Point Peron, which comprised two 155 mm mobile guns as well as two 18 pounder QF Mk II field guns. These guns were designed to work with the Challenger Battery to provide counter bombardment fire to the west of the island to protect Cockburn sound. In late 1943 these were replaced by the Collie Section based at Collie Head on Garden Island which was made up of two 12 pounder Mk I guns. The control of this network of defences of Cockburn Sound was undertaken by HQ Southern Fire Command which was established in January 1943.

By the time war broke out it was acknowledged that air power was indeed a threat and the early victories of the Japanese particularly against Pearl Harbour, the Philippines, and a host of other unfortunate victims highlighted just how serious this threat was. As a result, the air defences around

Fortress Fremantle were indeed formidable to support the coastal defence batteries.

First and foremost were fighter planes that were based at Pearce and Guildford air bases and these were supported by radars along the coast designed to detect incoming aircraft to enable the fighters to scramble and intercept them before they reached the harbour which was their priority target area. The Fremantle target area was a gun-controlled area and fighter controllers maintained close liaison with the anti-aircraft Ops Room.

The main gun used by the Australian and British armies for air defence in World War II was the 3.7 inch heavy anti-aircraft (AA) gun and it had an effective ceiling height of just under 10,000 metres. They were generally deployed in a group of four which was called a gun station or a 'troop'. Each gun station had a command post comprising a height and range finder and an aircraft recognition telescope, to attempt to avoid shooting down friendly aircraft. After determining the height of the attacking planes, the fuses would be set for the shells to explode at the predicted height. The guns would not shoot at the aircraft directly, but rather explode the shell in front of them releasing shrapnel that the plane would fly through causing severe damage and ideally, causing the aircraft to crash. There was a battery headquarters established for every four gun stations.

In dire circumstances, these guns could also operate in a secondary role and, from their positions, be brought down to operate in a horizontal position and fire seawards to engage targets. The 3.7 inch heavy anti-aircraft guns were about the same size and calibre as the famous 88 mm anti-aircraft gun which the German Army used with devastating effect against targets in a horizontal capacity. There were several gun stations each with four guns, the primary ones being at Garden Island (north and south), Buckland Hill Mosman Park, South Beach, East Fremantle Oval and North Fremantle Oval. There was also a troop based at the Fremantle Golf Course, whose role it was to defend the oil storage tanks from attack.

Supplementing the heavy anti-aircraft batteries were highly mobile 40 mm Bofors guns. These could be moved around quite quickly as needed and gave protection to the heavier flak guns by firing directly at low flying aircraft that might be coming in to attack the defences. The Bofors had a rate of fire of 120 rounds a minute, so it presented a significant threat to an attacking plane.

In addition to these were an array of lighter weapons for anti-aircraft defence, the primary ones being heavy mounted machine guns, primarily Vickers or Browning, which could shoot a stream of bullets towards oncoming aircraft to supplement the 1 kg shells of the Bofors guns. These were usually dug in to an emplacement alongside the heavy anti-aircraft batteries, or were mobile, being mounted on the back of a truck where they could easily and quickly be moved to support areas where existing defences had been knocked out, or where it was deemed their support was needed.

Given the threat of night attack, there were an abundance of anti-aircraft searchlight stations ranging from Swanbourne, down the coast to Point Peron and inland as far as Attadale and South Perth.

A coastal gun at Point Peron, part of Fortress Fremantle.

Aircraft over Rottnest Island.

Leighton Battery in Fremantle.

The Dauntless dive bomber in action.

Preparing a dive-bomber for action aboard the USS *Hornet*.

An anti-aircraft gun in the Pacific.

The bombing of Pearl Harbour.

OLIVER HILL BATTERY ROTTNEST ISLAND: THE GATEKEEPERS OF FREMANTLE

The battery that was established at Oliver Hill was originally going to be based at Buckland Hill, Mosman Park, until it was determined that the range from there would not be sufficient to deter a large ship firing on Fremantle from a distance. So it was decided that the more suitable position would be Rottnest Island, approximately 18 kilometres off the coast of Fremantle. This battery consisted of two 9.2 inch power operated counter bombardment guns that were capable of firing a 170 kg armour piercing shell a distance of 28.5 kilometres.

This battery would almost certainly have been the first to come in to contact with any invading forces or hostile ship, as the approach to Fremantle would have come from the north, to where these guns were sighted. Under extreme battle conditions they had a rate of fire of three shells per minute, and the accuracy of these guns, with a skilled crew would be to hit the target approximately once with every nine shots fired at the maximum range of 28.5 kilometres.

Below the battery, in concrete reinforced underground facilities was the power house, comprising two Ruston Hornsby diesel engines, battery fire control plotting rooms, a hydraulic pump chamber, separate magazines for both cordite and shells, and first aid casualty bays, all interconnected with underground tunnels.

Setting up these guns was a massive undertaking, and a Lieutenant, BF Hussey of the Royal Australian Engineers was given the job. Thousands of tonnes of raw materials needed to be shipped over to the island and the overall construction took almost three years. This included the building of a new jetty and a railway linking the jetty to the Oliver Hill site before construction on the guns could even commence. Given that the hill was basically a large sand dune, it was impossible to tunnel through it so in the end the top was dug off, the tunnels, magazine chambers and engine rooms were built, then the roofs reinforced before the sand and vegetation was put back on top of them. Although it was a large undertaking, labour was plentiful coming off the back of the depression.

Nearby, at Signal Ridge close to the main light-house, was a four-storey battery command post, which contained the range finding and other equipment to pass fire direction to the plotting rooms below the guns where the course of the battle would be observed and subsequently to the gunners above to determine the coordinates for their next firing. The battery command post could also post information direct to any other battery within the Fremantle Fortress System.

The battery command post was operated by the Australian Women's Army Services (AWAS) personnel. This was due to the greater ability of women to multitask in high pressure situations and, given that an attacking battleship would direct its fire at anything that might resemble a battery observation post to take away the gun batteries eyes, this would have been the case if the guns were ever attacked.

The Oliver Hill Gun Battery, World War 11.

THE SUBMARINES AND SHIPS
OF FREMANTLE HARBOUR

U p to 170 submarines were based at Fremantle in World War II and these were from the United States, Great Britain and Holland. They initially fled there after their bases in the Philippines, Singapore and Malaya along with the Dutch East Indies were overrun by the Japanese, and then continued to receive new submarines as the war progressed. Over the course of the war they operated throughout the Indian Ocean and into the waters of South East Asia as far north as the South China Sea. Although the coastal defences of Fremantle as shown were considerable, many ships also occupied the port. A large variety of destroyers and corvettes were based at the port to provide escort duties to the submarine fleet as well as convoys and assisting other naval maritime activities. In addition, the light cruiser, HMAS *Adelaide* spent almost the entire war based at Fremantle where she regularly escorted convoys. The *Adelaide* had a company of 26 officers and 436 sailors and sported considerable armament including nine of the BL 6 inch Mk XII naval guns as well as anti-aircraft guns and machine guns. In addition, she had two submerged 21 inch torpedo launchers. Launched in 1918, she had an extensive refit in 1938 and 1939 to prepare her for the modern age of warfare and her anti-aircraft armaments were improved. This was further upgraded in 1942 at the naval base in Sydney and consequently she was one of the vessels in Sydney harbour at the time of the Japanese midget submarine attack on 31 May 1942. This refit was completed in July 1942, at which point she was sent to Fremantle for convoy escort work.

In her time at Fremantle she worked alongside a Dutch light cruiser, the HNLMS *Jacob van Heemskerck*. A much more modern ship than the *Adelaide*, she was laid down in September 1939 and was hastily commissioned on 10 May 1940 when Germany invaded the Netherlands. However, due to the fact that she was not fully completed, she retreated to the United Kingdom where she was refitted as an air defence cruiser, these being the only types of guns available as everything else had been allocated to the forces of Great Britain and the Commonwealth. Fortunately, there was a growing need for this type of cruiser to protect convoys after the much-increased prevalence of air attacks in this new form of naval warfare that was gradually taking over the traditional war at sea.

Prior to arriving in Fremantle, in late May 1940 the *Heemskerck* and her sister ship the HNLMS *Sumatra*, were given an assignment by Queen Wilhelmina to transport Princess Juliana and her two children (including the Crown Princess) to Canada. She left Portsmouth on 2 June and arrived in Halifax on 11 June. In January 1942 she was sent to the Dutch East Indies to reinforce the defence fleet there amid growing concern over Japan who had recently bombed Pearl Harbour, invaded the Philippines and were heading down the Malayan Peninsula. She arrived too late to take part in the battle of the Java Sea on 27 February 1942, which was a major victory for the Japanese navy over the Allies, and she was reassigned to the Eastern Fleet. In September 1942, the ship took part in operations 'Stream' and 'Jane' which were aimed at the retaking of Madagascar. On 25 October 1942, *Heemskerck* arrived at Fremantle where she came under the command of the Allied Naval Forces of Western Australia and began her convoy escort duties alongside HMAS *Adelaide*.

Fremantle was the biggest submarine base in the southern hemisphere in World War II. Along with the *Bullhead*, in August 1945, the last US naval vessel to be lost in the war, many other American submarines that emanated from Fremantle were also sunk. These were *Grenadier*, *Grayling*, *Cisco* and *Capelin* in 1943. *Robalo*, *Flier*, *Hander* and *Growler* in 1944. *Barbel* and *Lagarto* joined *Bullhead* as lost submarines in 1945.

Fremantle Submarine Base

Submarines being prepared for patrol in Fremantle Harbour.

HMAS *Adelaide*

HMAS *Hobart*

LIFE IN FREMANTLE
DURING WORLD WAR II

When Japan attacked Pearl Harbour on 7 December 1941, the American response was swift. President Franklin Roosevelt immediately declared war on Japan and the next day, Australia joined them. The Australian Prime Minister John Curtin said at the time 'Australia goes to its battle stations in defence of its very way of living'. From that moment on, Curtin faced a significant number of difficulties. In February 1942 he saw the fortress of Singapore fall, Britain's naval stronghold and the principal line of defence for Australia. He saw the air raids across the north of the country and the closeness of the Japanese threat to Australia with the Battle of the Coral Sea. In 1943 he introduced conscription to Australia for the very first time in the country's history, and despite his own Labor Party's strong opposition to the very same measure in the First World War. Curtin is most remembered for putting in place Australia's wartime alliance with the United States and his decision to turn to America for help in 1942. In March that year, following the fall of Singapore, he warned the Americans that Australia was its last chance of defence against future raids upon the United States West Coast. This decision to side with America was not an easy one given Australia's longstanding Commonwealth association with Britain and it led to numerous heated arguments between Curtin and Winston Churchill. Ultimately, Churchill's decision not to seek to defend Australia against Japan, but to sacrifice it in the hope of building up defences against what he regarded as the more valuable Commonwealth asset, India, made Curtin's decision somewhat easier. Although it certainly led him to many sleepless nights and other health problems due to the stress of early 1942.

A number of Allied military and naval bases were established around Australia including Fremantle, and between 1942 and 1945, almost a million American servicemen were based in Australia. This was on top of Dutch and British servicemen who had found themselves in Australia as the Japanese swept south and overran their previous bases.

At home, the Australian population nervously watched events occur in the Asia Pacific region and wondered what the future held for their country. The loss of Singapore was a major blow to Australia's defensive plans and what dealt a major blow to the morale of the Australian population was learning that upon the fall of Singapore more than 15,000 Australian soldiers were taken prisoner. The loss of these servicemen and the knowledge that the bulk of the rest of the Australian army were in North Africa fighting against the German Army led by the mythical Field Marshall Erwin Rommel only increased the anxiety.

Shortly after the fall of Singapore, Japan bombed Darwin and over the following weeks conducted raids against Broome, Wyndham and Derby as well as other West Australian towns. These raids were carried out by planes launched from four large Japanese aircraft carriers in the Timor Sea. The people of Fremantle were convinced that it was only a matter of time before Fremantle was hit by Japan's advance. Efforts intensified by the military in Fremantle to prepare adequate defences which included barbed wire along most of the beaches, obstacles put in the water to prevent a beach landing by enemy soldiers and the rapid expansion of the anti-aircraft facilities.

Households in Fremantle were taught how to prepare for invasion or an air raid. Sheets were dyed black and hung across windows to black them out at night time. Businesses along High Street removed glass from their shopfronts and sandbagged the front of their stores as they boarded up their windows. Petrol rationing was brought in and those who were able to drive were forced to cover their head-lights at night time. People built air raid shelters in their back yards. Some resembled Britain's corrugated steel Anderson shelters standing tall, while others were dug into the ground and covered over. Several public spaces were also converted into air raid shelters and school playgrounds became criss-crossed with trenches for the local population to dive into and seek shelter in the event of an air raid.

Fremantle hospital was evacuated, and the patients were sent to Heathcote in Applecross and to Claremont so that Fremantle could be freed up to use as a casualty clearing station and first aid post in the event of an air raid or seaborne assault. South Terrace School, Princess May

Girls School and Fremantle Boys School were closed, and the students sent to Cottesloe, Palmyra and Bicton, which were all deemed to be away from the area of immediate risk if Fremantle were attacked. These schools struggled to cope with the increased numbers so school days were often split with some students attending school in the morning and others in the afternoon. When not in school, students were used to collect scrap metal to assist with the war effort.

Following the fall of Singapore in February 1942, and after Curtin's plea for American help, Australia became home to an increasing number of American servicemen including General Douglas MacArthur, who based himself in Australia after the fall of the Philippines, seeing the country as an increasingly important springboard to take the fight back up to the Japanese in the Pacific. By August 1942, more than 100,000 US personnel were here and a year later the number peaked at about 120,000. With Fremantle being the second biggest submarine base after Pearl Harbour, with around 170 American, Dutch and British submarines, more than 5,000 servicemen from these countries joined the existing Australian garrison. These servicemen found a welcoming community and as a result their morale was high. The hospitality and sense of belonging fostered by Western Australians towards these young men became legendary among the Allied submariners and remains central to the strength of the military relationship to this day. It did present some challenges, predominately a shortage of housing and food rationing, but after the Japanese air raids in the north of Australia, few complained about the protection they provided.

To the local population, the Americans were charming, well-mannered and friendly. They would be invited to dinner with local families and dances and other activities were organised to entertain them. Young children would roam around looking for Americans to offer to shine their shoes in exchange for the assorted flavours of Wrigley's gum that they possessed. The older kids if lucky might get a packet of Lucky Strike or Camel cigarettes, which were considered delicacies.

Australia-wide, unsurprisingly, tensions did occur between the two countries though, particularly as relationships began to develop between Australian women and American servicemen. Australian men fighting in the Pacific or Middle East would read with anger reports of married women having affairs with Americans. The Japanese propaganda machine sought to exploit this by claiming that American men were stealing Australian women while their husbands were away. These tensions were most common in the cities where there were particularly high numbers of Allied personnel. Brisbane was the standout as nearly 90,000 Americans became based there after MacArthur made this his primary base in 1942. The authorities tried to segregate the Australians and Americans to different parts of the city, but this did not stop the trouble and it came to a head in the 'Battle of Brisbane' in November 1942. In this two nights of rioting and fighting between Australian and American servicemen through the Queensland city on 26 – 27 November, one Australian was killed, and hundreds of Australian and United States soldiers were injured. Differences in pay and access to goods and services, such as the plentiful chocolates, cigarettes, ice-cream and hams available to the Americans, but luxuries to the Australians were the main causes of this.

Western Australia was not spared either and in January 1944 a riot involving a thousand American troops broke out in Perth's Hay Street causing substantial damage and terrified the local population. In April that year a brawl erupted between American and New Zealand troops in Fremantle's High Street in which two New Zealanders died.

Overall though, given the world tensions and the sheer number of Americans who passed through Australia, which was upwards of one million over its course, relationships were good and in Fremantle they remained excellent.

The submarine tender USS *Athedon* is waved off at Fremantle.

John Curtin, Prime Minister of Australia 1941 - 1945

THE ROLE OF SUBMARINES
IN THE PACIFIC WAR

The importance of the Port of Fremantle, as a submarine base, to the Allied war effort against Japan, is largely overlooked by history. By the beginning of 1945, the ability of Japan to provide raw materials for its industries and food for its population was critically paralysed. It was unable to import even a fraction of its requirements due to an invisible ring of steel surrounding it, which was created by the submarines of the US navy. Over the course of 1944, a significant amount of Japan's merchant shipping and even more significantly its tanker fleet had been sent to the bottom of the ocean. Yet the submarine force which did this received far less prominence than Nimitz's formidable carrier task groups with their multitudes of ships and planes or the marines landing on Iwo Jima or Okinawa, even though it imposed an economic strangulation on Japan that Germany was unable to do to Britain. In fact, a report by General MacArthur's headquarters in April 1945 stated, 'The entire question of Japanese merchant shipping requirements may soon be academic, if losses continue at anything like the present rate'. Only 16,000 men, or 1.6 percent of the US navy's strength served on submarines, although they accounted for 55 percent of all of Japan's wartime shipping losses. A total of 1,300 Japanese vessels including cruisers, battleships and aircraft carriers were sunk as well as the decimation of the merchant fleet, which all up weighed a total of 6.1 million tonnes.

The Japanese empire was uniquely vulnerable to blockade. Its economy was reliant on fuel and raw materials shipped in from China, Malaya, Burma and the Netherlands East Indies. However, unlike Britain, who was in a similar situation, being an island and totally reliant on an Atlantic lifeline, the Japanese failed to defend their commerce by putting in place an efficient anti-submarine deterrent. This was one of the major causes of Japan's downfall, the fixing of the minds of her Admirals on the projection of power by surface and air forces. Japan possessed only a small number of anti-submarine escorts whose technology and tactics remained obsolete.

At the outbreak of the Second World War, the United States had in its possession the finest submarines in the world, the 1500 tonne *Tambor*-class, to be later refined even further as the *Gato* and *Balao* classes. First and foremost, they had air-conditioning, something worth its weight in gold when operating in the tropics. They had a top speed of 21 knots, a range of 18,000 kilometres and the ability to crash dive in 35 seconds. The only reason they were not as effective early in the war was due to chronic torpedo technical failure, and incredibly overly cautious commanders who were aghast at the thought of accidentally sinking in error a non-combatant ship due to misidentification, and subsequently missing legitimate targets. Most of these men had been dismissed by the end of 1942 to be replaced by a new breed of young and aggressive commanders. As it was, only in 1944 did America's campaign against Japanese commerce begin in earnest after the shortcomings of its torpedos had been eventually addressed, and the deployments of the submarines much better directed.

During World War II, Germany lost 781 submarines, and Japan lost 128. By comparison, the Japanese navy managed to sink only 41 American submarines. Six more were accidentally lost on patrols in the Pacific and in the South China Sea. Even these humble losses meant that 22 percent of all US submariners perished – 375 officers and 3,131 enlisted men – making this the highest loss rate of any of the branches of US armed forces. Despite this, there was never a shortage of volunteers for the submarine service, with its remarkable pride and old-fashioned buccaneering spirit. Although receiving a 50 percent premium on their base pay, matching that paid to aviators, it was not just the money that kept them signing up. It was the feeling that they genuinely were part of an elite force. On top of this was the informality aboard the submarine compared to other services. Men manned their station in shorts and grew beards if they wanted to. They ate whenever they felt like it – the submarine adopted an 'open icebox' policy. There was a little authorised drinking aboard and some men smuggled their own alcohol aboard or made it when they got there. So apart from the strict operational disciplines maintained when at battle stations, most of the time life aboard was fairly relaxed. These operational disciplines at the right moment were the key to survival though because for those who manned these stinking underwater torpedo platforms, the only thing that matched the thrill and exhilaration of hunting their quarry, was the sheer terror they themselves experienced when they became the hunted.

Unlike popular belief that they spent most of their time underwater, submarines were almost always on the surface of the water where they could move more swiftly than most convoys. Their normal procedure was to shadow the enemy vessels until they could make their attack under the cover of darkness. When night fell it was often possible to attack while the submarine was still on the surface, which was the preferred tactic. If they did choose to submerge to make their attack, the captain bent over the periscope lens underneath the conning tower calculating ranges and calling off details of the target and orders for the approach. The captains were taught that surprise is fundamental. Use the periscope as little as possible, and remember that the higher your underwater speed, the more noticeable the periscopes wake would be. Never just fire into a convoy, always pick a ship and aim for it. Set a salvo of torpedos to run in a spread that should cover 80 percent of the vessels length. The straighter the firing angle, the better the chances of scoring a hit. The ruination of every attacking submarine skipper was the sudden change of course of the target which is why every prudent surface ship zigzagged, notwithstanding the inherent difficulties associated with getting a massive convoy to zigzag in unison.

One of the reasons Japan's submarines never enjoyed the success of the Americans is that for much of the war they were given the job of transporting supplies to beleaguered garrisons of troops spread throughout islands across the Pacific and South East Asia. The Imperial Japanese Navy had far better torpedos than the Americans, but their commanders were much less aggressive. Nimitz's US captains were young tigers by comparison. The Admirals of the American submarine fleet had absolutely no patience for timidity. Any captain who seemed to lack aggression was sacked on the spot. Lack of aggression meaning basically coming home without sinking any enemy ships. In 1944, 35 out of 250 skippers were dismissed for the cardinal sin of 'non-productivity'.

After completing an attack, a submarine either fled at full speed or, if in danger of being spotted by escorts, which it often was, it went deep. Destroyers could travel at least 15 knots faster than a submarine using its diesel engines on the surface and much more against a submerged submarine dependent on its electric motors. Captains were instructed, never try and fight it out on the surface. A single deck gun was insufficient defence against a heavily armed destroyer and a shrapnel or shell hit to the hull of a submarine could prevent its ability to submerge. Being depth charged was a terrifying experience for all the men aboard a submarine, as they sat in darkness listening to the explosions unleashed against them by warships groping away for their underwater victim. An American boat would seek refuge far beneath the surface, hopefully in a friendly thermal current which would deflect sonar signals, and with all its non-essential equipment shut down to reduce the submarines sound profile. With the air-conditioners shut off, the atmosphere in the hull grew fouler by the minute and perspiration poured down the men's bodies. Only as the sound of the depth charging began to become more distant, as the destroyer changed its search pattern away from the silent sub, did tensions slowly begin to ease.

A tragic side to the submarine war was that it cost the lives of around 10,000 Allied prisoners as Nimitz's commanders had no way of identifying if the Japanese transports they were lining up in their sights were carrying prisoners. The US Navy adopted a ruthless view in this regard, that destruction of the enemy must take priority over any effort to safeguard the lives of the prisoners of war. There was no way this could not have been the case. If the Japanese had determined that efforts were being made to protect POW lives, they would simply have loaded every transport with prisoners to be 'human shields' to prevent the ships being sunk. Nevertheless, the euphoria of sinking a transport was often tempered by the knowledge that it could have been carrying prisoners being transported back to the Japanese islands for slave labour.

The most successful US submarine of the Second World War was the *Flasher*, a *Gato*-class submarine who was well known to Fremantle, having spent considerable time in the port both resting and refitting after her war patrols into the South China Sea and the Pacific. She achieved 21 sinkings totalling over 100,000 tonnes. On her fifth war patrol, in December 1944, after departing Fremantle on 15 November, she accounted for four tankers and two destroyers between the Philippines and Indochina. Each carried 100,000 barrels of oil and only 300,000 barrels ended up reaching Japan that month. Thus, this one submarine managed to cut Japan's December oil imports by two thirds. On that same patrol, off the coast of Indochina on 22 December she managed to despatch three more tankers. Such was the incredible effect of the blockade and the men who controlled the submarines that executed it.

After the war, in 1946, the US Strategic Bombing survey was completed. This survey, which it would have been expected to be highly unlikely to reach any conclusion that might be biased in favour of the navy did in fact conclude and declare 'The war against shipping was the most decisive single factor in the collapse of the Japanese economy and logistic support of Japanese military and naval power. Submarines accounted for the majority of vessel sinkings'. There was no other combatant force anywhere in the world, as small as the US navy's submarine fleet and its 16,000 men, that achieved a comparable impact and had such a massive effect on the final outcome.

THE END OF THE
BATTLESHIP ERA

Although the defences of Rottnest Island and the surrounding coastline of Fremantle Harbour would have presented a daunting target to any would-be attacker, the reality is that by the early 1940s when Australia was seriously threatened, the very nature of war had dramatically changed. The huge battleships that had roamed the seas for decades, and that the batteries that had been put in place to defend Fremantle against attack, were already obsolete, as navies could launch planes now from aircraft carriers hundreds of miles away to pinpoint and destroy a target. Although military leaders of the time had not completely grappled with this fact, and still put their face in their huge warships bristling with guns, the day of the battleship was over and any attack against Fremantle Harbour would most likely have commenced from the air, in the same way as Darwin had been bombed in early 1942.

Battleships themselves, even though armed to the teeth with anti-aircraft guns and machine guns to protect them from air attack, were finding themselves no match for a determined attack from skilful aviators with canon, bombs and torpedos.

Interestingly, it was some members of the Japanese Armed Forces who led the race in understanding that the days of the battleships were numbered in light of new advances in aviation technology. The Japanese naval air corps had over the years of 1937 – 1941 shown its growing power and range over the skies of China, where it maintained absolute mastery of the air over the expanse of that country. The more powerful and successful the air arm grew, the more the confidence grew of the of the aviation officers within it that the navy should reduce its emphasis on battleships, and from now on devote the bulk of its vast resources to building more airplanes and aircraft carriers. Lieutenant Commander Minoru Genda, whilst on a tour of duty at the naval general staff in Tokyo in 1936, wrote a report where he provocatively stated that 'the main strength of a decisive battle should be air arms, while battleships should be put out of commission and tied up'. He not only wanted to stop building battleships altogether but, committing almost heresy in this island country, suggested that all existing ones 'should be either scrapped or used as hulks for jetties'. These comments were complete sacrilege, profanation and provocation. The entire navy's basic battle instruction stated: 'the battleship squadron is the main fleet, whose aim is to attack and destroy the enemy's main fleet'. Genda's rivals, and there were many of them, spread rumours that he had lost his mind, with some even suggesting that he should be committed to an asylum.

Genda's problem was, that owing to the tradition of the navy and the relatively new field of air arms, very few aviation-minded officers occupied posts in the overall naval command structure. Most of the officers who saw the future of naval war through aviation were lower ranking and simply could not make themselves heard to the traditionalists who could not imagine an airplane being anything more than a minor inconvenience to a battleship. Genda did, however, find a partner and a patron in the form of Admiral Yamamoto himself, who is widely regarded as the greatest admiral since the English Lord Nelson. Yamamoto ensured that the young man was given the assignments he wanted and made him one of his principal staff officers in the combined fleet in 1940. Yamamoto also openly expressed his doubts about the future of the battleship and rejected the notion that there was any such thing as an unsinkable ship.

He also argued that with aviation development, planes would have even longer ranges and steadily growing offensive power, further contributing to the decline of the battleship. In a conversation with Rear Admiral Keiji Fukuda, an ardent battleship man, Yamamoto stated, 'I don't want to be a wet blanket, and I know you're going all out on your job, but I'm afraid you'll be out of work before long. From now on, aircraft are going to be the most important thing in the navy; big ships and guns will become obsolete'.

Fukuda, and his legion of big gun battleship supporters in the navy were not going to allow a bunch of impertinent aviators to have any control over the future of the Japanese navy. Anticipating that Japan would renege on its treaty obligations regarding ship sizes when it expired in 1936, the Naval General Staff commenced plans to build a fleet of 'superbattleships'. The ships would weigh 64,000 tonnes and be 50 percent larger than anything that the Americans had in their fleet. Their main battery would be guns of 18.1 inch calibre. The navy's argument was that with weapons of such range and armament they would win any engagement with an enemy fleet no matter how many ships they came up against on the other side. If they laid the keels immediately, they could commence construction of the ships immediately upon the treaty's expiry and that would potentially give them a five-year advantage over their rivals in Britain and the United States. The ships would of course be built under closely guarded secrecy, but even if the Americans got wind of what they were doing and began building their own battleships of matching size, they would be too broad beamed to pass through the Panama Canal and would have to round the Horn to get to Japan. Setting out at the same time if war broke out, the Japanese 'superbattleships', departing from their ports in Yokosuka or Kure could potentially be arriving in San Francisco Bay before the Atlantic based American ships had even reached the bottom of South America.

So, in 1936 the navy placed its initial order for two of the ships to be built. The ship builders were astounded by the specifications they received to build these ships, which were to be 263 metres long and 38.9 metres on the beam. Their steam turbined engines would deliver 150,000 horse-power, which would have the ability to drive them through the sea at a speed of 27 knots. They would carry a 2,500-man crew and 6,300 tonnes of fuel giving them a range of

7,200 nautical miles. It was believed that shells fired at them or bombs dropped from above would have no impact on them due to their 40 cm thick armour plating of a unique 'honeycomb' design. In addition, the hull would have 1,147 watertight compartments, meaning that if they were hit by shells or torpedoes, they were all capable of being sealed off to contain flooding. According to the navy they would be 'unsinkable'! Until that is they were sunk in 1944 and 1945.

The ships were to be named the *Yamato*, which was to be built at the Port of Kure, in Hiroshima and the *Musashi*, to be built in Nagasaki. The Japanese went to extraordinary lengths to ensure the secrecy of the construction of these battleships because they worried that if the Americans got wind of what they were doing they would immediately begin building ships of a similar size. Large fences were erected around the Mitsubishi shipyard, ferries traversing workers in the harbour had their windows painted black so that commuters could not inadvertently glance in the direction of the shipyards and police swarmed the streets threatening to arrest anyone who even appeared to glance in the direction of the mighty ship being built. This was no easy task in a place such as Nagasaki, which was a city of hills, with any number of vantage points were people could potentially peer down at the mighty gargantuan slowly taking shape in its dock. Any plans and documents in relation to the ships were forbidden to leave the shipyard offices.

So big were these ships that the interiors were a vast maze of passageways and ladders. Very few workers actually knew their way around the ships. As no plans were provided to the workers due to the strict secrecy of the project, they had to make do with their own crude maps which had to be destroyed at the end of each day, with some even drawing maps of the layout on their arms to enable themselves to find their way around. They also took pieces of chalk to draw trails so that they could find their way back at the end of the day.

The *Yamato* was launched on 8 August 1940 without incident at the Port of Kure. The launch of the *Musashi* on 1 November 1940 however was not so easy. The harbour of Nagasaki was very narrow with steep land on either side. As *Musashi* entered the water she would be travelling at a speed of 15 knots. The opposite shore was only 720 metres away so unless the speed could be slowed she ran the risk of hitting it and destroying an entire neighbourhood as well as herself. In the end, the engineers rigged heavy chains to the side of her to turn her as she entered the water, as well as running cables from harbour moorings to her hull to slow her down. So secretive was the launch that all residents were ordered to remain indoors with their curtains drawn and only thirty guests, all high ranking naval and government officials were invited to it.

As the ship crashed into the water on its launch it created a giant wave which swept to the other side and flooded a number of buildings, as well as capsizing a myriad of boats, but the launch had succeeded. The engineers and the workers fell to the ground weeping with joy and shouting thanks to the heavens.

The ships underwent their sea trials and performed perfectly. When the guns were tested for the first time on the *Musashi* the 18.1 inch guns threw their armour piercing projectiles, each weighing 1.5 tonnes, to a maximum range of 42 kilometres. A shell fired from that range with a gun elevation of 45 degrees effectively climbed from sea level to the tip of Mount Everest and back to sea level again, the flight of the shell lasting nearly two minutes. Any battleship on the receiving end of this colossal shell would immediately be put out of action if not destroyed and a smaller ship would simply be annihilated and sent to the bottom of the ocean.

The *Musashi* was sunk by 19 torpedos and 17 bomb hits from planes from US aircraft carriers on 24 October 1944 in the battle of Leyte Gulf. The *Yamato* was sunk by 11 torpedoes and six bombs, also from American carrier-based aircraft on 7 April 1945 in the Japanese navy's response to the invasion of Okinawa.

The unsinkable ships, both of which were built in defiance of a new generation of thinking that air power was the way of the future, went to the bottom at the hands of the very aircraft that they were built in defiance of. But the Japanese were not alone in their arrogance towards the growing danger posed by the threat from the skies. Many years earlier, as war raged along the Malayan Peninsula, Britain had lost two of her finest battleships at the hands of air power.

Japanese Admiral Isoroku Yamamoto

The *Yamato* was one of the most powerful battleships ever built.

THE REPULSE AND THE
PRINCE OF WALES

Shortly before Pearl Harbour, Prime Minister Churchill, concerned about possible Japanese aggression towards Singapore, had ordered a naval squadron, 'Force Z' to the colony as a deterrent. Force Z was built around two of the Royal Navy's finest ships, the battleship *Prince of Wales* and the battlecruiser *Repulse*. The ultimate fate of these two ships, perhaps even more than the damage inflicted at Pearl Harbour, was to mark a new chapter in naval history.

On 8 December 1941, only hours after the attack on Pearl Harbour, Admiral Tom Phillips, the commander of Force Z, ordered his squadron to intercept a Japanese invasion fleet which had been sighted north of Malaya in the South China Sea. Force Z was without any air cover as the aircraft carrier which had originally been proposed to accompany the fleet, the HMS *Indomitable*, had run aground in the Caribbean Sea. The British, perhaps holding an exaggerated belief in the power of the battleship, an attitude certainly held by

Churchill, had decided to push on regardless. Phillips was aware of this danger but was hopeful that the operation could be finished quickly so that Force Z could get away eastward before the Japanese would be able to 'mass a formidable scale of attack against us'.

From the outset, Force Z ran into problems. It suffered difficulty in even locating the Japanese fleet that it was searching for. It headed into the Gulf of Siam toward the beachhead that had been established by the Japanese invading force near Kota Bahru in the north of Malaya. It then headed down the coast in pursuit of what turned out to be a false report of another Japanese landing near Kuantan, about 150 miles away.

Although they were without air cover, the crews and the officers aboard these two large vessels remained very confident. Although they had heard reports that had filtered through about the terrific losses sustained by the British Air Force in the air battles over northern Malaya, and the devastating attack on the American battleships only the day before at the hands of the Japanese Air Force, they maintained an absolute faith that the Japanese, whether navy or air force, could not possibly be any match for two of the Royal Navy's best, and most powerful ships. In fact, the main topic of conversation occurring between the seamen onboard the ships, was how long it would take them to sink the Japanese warships they knew would be somewhere around Singora in northern Malaya. Bert Wynn, an able seaman on board the *Repulse* remarked, 'I still remember the feeling of absolute confidence running throughout the ship...the outcome of such an engagement was felt to be a formality'. On 9 December at around 1600 hours, when a

British patrol plane came across a Japanese surface force, an officer on board the *Repulse* remarked to Cecil Brown, who was a CBS radio correspondent and happened to be on the ship at the time as a press observer, 'Oh but they are Japanese. There is nothing to worry about'.

Brown was quite perturbed by this comment and later that evening over dinner in the officers' mess raised the question, in light of what had happened at Pearl Harbour, were the British not being too confident. The British officers considered the question deliberately and carefully. Eventually one conceded that it was 'wrong' to underestimate the enemy, but then another officer replied, which perhaps summed up the arrogance that still existed within the admiralty, 'we are not overconfident; we just don't think the enemy is much good. They could not beat China for five years and now look what they are doing out here, jumping all over the map instead of meeting at one or two places. They cannot be very smart to be doing that'.

The air attack on Force Z began just after 1100 hours on the morning of 10 December. The Japanese planes had spread out to search for their targets, so they arrived upon the task force in small groups. The first wave of planes, consisting of Nell bombers from the Mihoro Air Corps, concentrated their attack solely on the Repulse. Despite having seven near misses with their 250 kg bombs, they scored one hit which penetrated the hangar and the upper deck exploding in the mess area. Despite killing around 20 sailors, the explosion caused no severe damage and the ship continued. Five of the eight bombers were hit by the ships anti-aircraft fire.

About half an hour later, the radar sets of the ships in Force Z picked up a flight of nine G3M torpedo bombers coming towards them. They approached the ships virtually just above the wavetops and this time they selected the Royal Navy's flagship, *Prince of Wales*, as their target. They dove on the target in packs of two or three, attacking the ship on both sides. They hit her twice near the stern, wrecking her rudder and flooding the engine room. The incapacitated ship continued to steam in an erratic circle, with smoke pouring into the sky above her.

A third attack then occurred, this time led by torpedo armed G4M's of the Kanoya Air Group and they selected the *Repulse* as their target. The ship, which had survived the first barrage, carried out numerous manoeuvres in an effort to save herself, managing to avoid about 20 torpedos in the process, but she was finally caught by the Japanese planes in a classic 'anvil' attack with torpedos dropped off both of her bows at the same time.

Cecil Brown, the CBS correspondent who watched the whole event occur from the flag deck, summed the attack up as follows; 'for me, this whole picture – orange flames belching from the four inchers, white tracers from pom poms and Vickers guns, and grey airplanes astonishingly close, like butterflies pinned on blue cardboard – is a confusing, macabre game'.

Repulse was struck four times and she immediately started to sink, within seconds taking a frightening list to port. The crew knew that she was lost, and no amount of counter flooding could right her. The captain ordered the immediate abandonment of the ship, shouting to his men 'you've put up a good show, now save yourselves'. The men jumped into the sea, where a large number drowned, and many others remained there, treading water for many hours. At 1223 hours the *Repulse* rolled over in the sea and sank stern first, her bow pointing to the sky as if gasping for her last breaths as she slid to her grave. British destroyers, desperately scanning the skies for any torpedo bombers still hanging around that might want to take a shot at them too, circled around the area where the *Repulse* had sunk in an effort to rescue the surviving sailors, their faces blackened from the fuel oil that lay thickly across the surface of the ocean.

Now that the *Repulse* was at the bottom of the sea, the next wave of Japanese bombers arrived and set about the task of putting away the severely crippled *Prince of Wales*. At 1244 hours, she was hit in her chimney area by a 500 kg bomb dropped by a G4M bomber. The ship began to sink immediately, trapping many of her sailors below deck when she rolled over. The destroyers continued manfully to circle the area picking up as many survivors as they possibly could whilst still on the lookout for any remaining planes or a new attack wave on the horizon. One Japanese plane which was leaving the area with the rest of the attack wave flew low over the tops of these destroyers and flashed a bravura taunt in plain English 'we have finished our mission now. You may carry on'.

The sinking of the *Repulse* and the *Prince of Wales* claimed the lives of 47 British officers and 793 sailors. Incredibly, the Japanese lost only three planes in the battle. The British, so arrogantly disregarding of the Japanese less than 24 hours before, were forced to admit that the attack had been carried out with textbook precision. The captain of the *Repulse* wrote after the battle 'the enemy attacks were without doubt magnificently carried out and pressed well home. The high-level bombers kept tight formation and appeared not to jink'. Indeed, the Japanese had done their homework and their training perfectly. The high-level bombers arrived first and distracted the anti-aircraft gunners and the torpedo bombers followed closely behind, came in low and dropped their torpedos in classic pincer attacks.

When Winston Churchill received the news by telephone, he stumbled to right himself as he asked Admiral Sir Dudley Pound in a shaking voice 'are you sure it's true?' 'There is no doubt at all' Pound replied. As Churchill replaced the phone back in to its cradle, he wrote later about the event: 'I was glad to be alone. In all of the war I never received a more direct shock....as I turned over and twisted in bed the full horror of the news sank in upon me.... over all this vast expanse of waters Japan was supreme, and we everywhere weak and naked'. The loss of these ships was a huge loss to British naval prestige. The *Prince of Wales*, in particular, was the newest and supposedly most formidable battleship in the fleet.

If anything, it was this engagement between aircraft and battleships that highlighted the rapidly changing face of warfare and that the mighty capital ships that had traversed the globe showing off their massive armaments were now largely obsolete in the face of aircraft launched from aircraft carriers or coastal air bases. The formidable defences of Fremantle Harbour would be more likely to come under air attack than battleships preceding an invasion fleet.

Escaping from *Prince of Wales* after air attack.

HMAS *SYDNEY*

Although the main threat to the continent of Australia during World War II came from Japan, who was engaged more directly in the Pacific Theatre, it was Germany who, not far from the Port of Fremantle, inflicted one of the nation's worst military disasters in terms of loss of life and military prestige with the sinking of the HMAS *Sydney*. The ship was sunk on the 19 November 1941 by the German raider *Kormoran* 280 kilometres south-west of Carnarvon. This was not an unusual place for a German ship to be and in fact many German vessels plied this coast line, particularly in the early stages of the war.

The *Sydney* was a modified Leander-class (or Perth-class) light cruiser which had been built for the Royal Navy. She was purchased for the Australian Government to replace HMAS *Brisbane* and was commissioned into the Royal Australian Navy in 1935. The cruiser was 562 feet long and carried eight 6 inch guns in four turrets as her primary armament. These were supplemented by four 4 inch anti-aircraft guns, nine .303 inch machine guns as well as eight 21 inch torpedo tubes in two quadruple mountings. Although initially given the task of escorting and patrol duties in Australian waters, the *Sydney* was sent to the Mediterranean in mid-1940. She operated against Italian naval forces for around eight months where she participated in a number of battles. She sank two Italian warships, several merchantmen and supported convoy operations and shore bombardments. In early January 1941, *Sydney* was recalled to Australia. The ship needed maintenance and refitting, and the personnel needed rest, and to facilitate the spreading of combat experience across the RAN fleet. Also, there was a strong desire to reinforce the country following a large amount of German raider activity, particularly along the West Australian coast. *Sydney* was assigned to Fremantle, and the command of the ship was handed over to Captain Joseph Burnett in May 1941.

The *Kormoran* was a merchant ship, originally named *Steiemark*, that was identified by the Germans as a ship that would be suitable for commerce raiding. During the 1930s the restrictions of the Treaty of Versailles forbade the Germans building large ships so other methods of arming a navy were needed. The Kriegsmarine took up the *Steiemark* at the start of World War II and renamed her *Kormoran*. She was the largest and the newest of nine of these raiders, who the Germans referred to as *Hilfskreuzer* (auxiliary cruisers) or *Handelsstorkreuzer* (trade disruption cruisers). The *Kormoran* was 515 feet long and was fitted with six single 5.9 inch guns, two each in the forecastle and quarterdeck, with the fifth and sixth on the centreline, and was supplemented by two 37 mm anti-tank guns, five 20 mm anti-aircraft cannons, and six 21 inch torpedo tubes.

The 5.9 inch guns were concealed behind false hull plates and cargo hatch walls. These could swing clear when the de-camouflage order was given. The ship's additional stealth was that she could be disguised as any one of a number of Allied or neutral vessels.

The *Sydney* carried a crew of 645 men: 41 officers, 594 sailors, 6 Royal Australian Air Force personnel, and four civilian canteen staff. The *Kormoran* carried 399 personnel: 36 officers, 359 sailors and four Chinese sailors hired from the crew of a captured merchantman to run the ship's laundry.

The *Kormoran* departed German waters in December 1940 under the command of Theodor Detmers. She initially operated in the Atlantic where she sank seven merchant ships and captured an eighth. She then sailed to the Indian Ocean in late April 1941. Carrying several hundred sea mines, the *Kormoran* was expected to deploy these prior to returning home to Germany in 1942. Detmers plan was to mine shipping routes near Cape Leeuwin and Fremantle, given the large increase in naval shipping in those locations, particularly submarine activity. However, after detecting wireless signals from an Australian warship, the heavy cruiser HMAS *Canberra* he decided to postpone that operation and instead head towards Shark Bay and investigate that area.

The *Sydney* departed Fremantle on 11 November heading towards Singapore with the transport SS *Zealandia*. These two vessels headed towards the Sunda Strait at which point the troopship was handed over to the HMS *Durban* on 17 November. *Sydney* then turned for home and was scheduled to arrive back in Fremantle on 20 November.

The *Kormoran* encountered the *Sydney* at about 1600 hours on 19 November. Detmers altered his course and built up to full speed while preparing the ship at battle stations. As the two ships came closer together, Burnett, on board the *Sydney* requested that the *Kormoran* identify itself, however, Detmers attempted to evade the question. The *Sydney* persisted, and after some considerable delay, the *Kormoran* gave the call sign for a Dutch merchantman *Straat Malakka* and hoisted an ensign. This subterfuge caused the *Sydney* to come in closer where it requested a clearer signal. The *Kormoran* did so, in the process swinging its halyard around to starboard to face the *Sydney*. The Australian ship now demanded to know where the *Kormoran* was bound, to which the reply was received 'Batavia' (Jakarta) which certainly fitted with the claims of the ship to be Dutch. Even more deception was received by the *Sydney* such as the *Kormoran's* port of origin being Fremantle and her cargo being 'piece goods'. The German ship's ruse was very well prepared and managed to deceive the Australians at every turn and breaking every rule of engagement on the high seas.

The ships continued to exchange messages which even further confused the situation including the claim that the *Kormoran* was a merchantman under attack. Surprisingly though, Captain Burnett still did not appear overly suspicious, perhaps because of the large amount of merchant shipping passing through the area at that time. The *Sydney* was positioned parallel to the raider off its starboard beam about 1,300 metres away. The *Sydney* was probably not even at 'action stations' at this point, although the Germans claimed that the main guns and the port torpedo launcher were aimed at them. Captain Detmers ordered his crew to prepare to engage.

At 1730 hours, when the German ship had failed to respond to another request from the *Sydney* for fifteen minutes, the Australian signalled that she should show her secret sign. Detmers refused and finally ordered his crew to reveal its true identification and the German flag was raised. At the same time the order was given for its guns and torpedo tubes to fire, the *Sydney* did the same. The two ships fired multiple salvos at each other, each of them scoring hits. A German torpedo struck the *Sydney*'s hull at its weakest point where it tore a massive hole in the side of the ship. This catastrophic damage caused the *Sydney*'s bow to angle down. Burnett turned the ship hard to port which Detmers interpreted as a sign that the Australians may be attempting to ram them, however, the *Sydney* passed behind the *Kormoran*. The Germans let loose a tenth salvo, scoring more hits and doing even more damage to their larger opponent.

The engagement lasted around five minutes. The *Sydney* faltered away to the south, its main weaponry was completely out of action and its secondary weapons out of the *Kormoran's* range. Numerous fires had broken out all over the ship. The *Kormoran* all the while kept firing its aft guns at the *Sydney* and continued scoring hits. At around 1745 hours, 15 minutes after the commencement of the fight, Detmers decided that he wanted to destroy *Sydney* completely. He ordered the *Kormoran* to swing to port so that he could fire four gun salvos. This turned out to be a good decision, it took the raider out of line of two of the *Sydney*'s torpedo tubes, however, just as it completed its turn, its engines failed, and it stopped motionless. In the meantime, the *Sydney* continued sailing south at an ever-reducing speed. Even while motionless the *Kormoran* continued to fire at her. In all, more than 450 shells were fired towards *Sydney*, with around half of these scoring hits on the vessel. At 1750 hours the *Sydney* was around six kilometres away and out of range of the raider. Detmers fired one final torpedo towards her but it missed the target.

The entire battle had lasted a mere half hour and the ships were now 10 kilometres apart. Both were on fire and severely damaged. At 1825 hours the German captain ordered his men to abandon ship and 317 of the 397-crew made it into life rafts and were rescued. The *Sydney* continued to drift for another six hours and the Germans in their life rafts could see her fires until midnight. At that time, the ship sank, upright. As it submerged, the bow broke off and descended almost vertically to the bottom. The rest of the hull glided 500 metres forward and then sank, stern first to the bottom. Of the 645 Australian personnel on board, no-one survived. It was Australia's worst naval disaster. *Kormoran* sank at about the same time as the *Sydney* when an explosion occurred in her hold at about 0030 hours.

On 23 November 1941, and with the *Sydney* not arrived in Fremantle, wireless communications stations sent out signals requesting her to report in. Before long, all the high power wireless stations around the country had joined in seeking a response. There was none, and the navy feared the worst. All ships in her last known area were ordered to search for her. A British tanker, the *Trocas*, found one of the *Kormoran's* life rafts and rescued the 25 German sailors on board it. Under interrogation, the Germans told of the fierce naval battle they had engaged in with an Australian ship which the navy assumed to be *Sydney*. The Australian Naval Board was informed of this on 24 November and it immediately contacted the Prime Minister, John Curtin.

Curtin was devastated by the loss of the ship and felt genuine pain for the families of the sailors on board. True to form he found a way to blame himself for the tragedy. The *Sydney*'s departure from Sydney to Fremantle had been delayed by industrial trouble. He had long had a reputation of being soft on trade unionists. Had this softness contributed to the ships loss? If he had been tougher with the unions perhaps the ship would have left on time and subsequently may have avoided the attack. Curtin confessed to the British governor-general, Lord Gowrie, that he did not have the nerve to make a public announcement to the nation about the probable loss of the entire crew. 'I couldn't bear to think about the shock the news would bring to relatives and friends of the crew' he told Gowrie. Gowrie told him to say nothing. German survivors from the *Kormoran* were still trickling in and indeed many had already been rescued. The *Sydney*'s crew was much larger and there was a good chance that some of them would also be found. However, pressure mounted on Curtin, the media wanted answers and rumours abounded as the crew members next of kin were sent customary telegrams informing them that their loved one was missing as a result of enemy action.

Finally, on 30 November, Curtin forced himself to make an official announcement about the fate of the *Sydney* and the loss of all hands. Newspapers could now publish the horrific news, although radio stations were ordered to wait for two days in case their broadcasts were heard by other German ships operating off the West Australian coast.

For the first time it dawned on the nation that Australia itself, not just Australian servicemen abroad, were very close to war. An atmosphere of doom descended across the country. France had fallen eighteen months before and now almost all of Europe was controlled by the Germans or by their Allies (Italy, Hungary, Bulgaria and Vichy France) or countries alleged to be friends with them (Spain, Finland and Sweden). The German Air Force had pounded England and in June 1941 a vast German army of three million men had invaded Russia in Operation Barbarossa and had seemingly effortlessly spread across the Ukraine capturing Kiev, they had surrounded Leningrad, and as the *Sydney* sank were approaching the gates of Moscow. Most Australians thought the war in Russia was virtually over.

In the pacific theatre Japan controlled Korea, Vietnam and a large part of northern and coastal China and were winning every battle against a Chinese army which seemed on the verge of collapse. Military observers felt that Chinese armed resistance would end by early 1942 and millions of Chinese had died in the fighting, or of atrocities at the hands of, the Japanese army. In fact, it seemed that nothing would stop the Japanese conquering China and then turning their attention to India. All the while, the trade embargo being mounted by the US against Japan was worrying many that some kind of conflict between America and Japan was also imminent.

The sinking of the HMAS *Sydney* could not have happened at a worse time for the morale of the Australian people and its government.

HMAS *Sydney*

THE RISE OF THE
AIRCRAFT CARRIER

Although the coastal gun fortifications defending Fremantle were indeed impressive, the reality is that they were already largely obsolete by the time the Second World War commenced. The battleships that had for decades ruled the waves and allowed countries to display their military might to the far reaches of the globe were now of secondary significance as air power grew in the effect that it could have and a new type of ship, the aircraft carrier, became the lynchpin of navies, particularly those of America and Japan.

The ability of aircraft to surge forward from either their land bases, or an aircraft carrier, and sink previously unsinkable ships was a new phenomenon that both armed forces and political powers were still grappling to come to terms with. No less significant events occurred than the sinking of the *Repulse* and the *Prince of Wales* off the coast of Malaya by Japanese bombers operating from the mainland; the sinking of the mighty German battleship, the *Bismark* by antiquated Fairey Swordfish biplanes carrying torpedoes from the deck of a British aircraft carrier, the *Ark Royal*, in the Atlantic, and of course the decimating attack on Pearl Harbour by planes of the Japanese air force operating from the decks of carriers nearby; an attack that could have been far more devastating and potentially altered the outcome of the war if the three US carriers based at Pearl Harbour had been in the harbour at that time.

Recognising this, aircraft carriers were quickly becoming the lynchpin of navies to be able to carry attack aircraft and launch them many miles ahead of a fleet to seek out and destroy the enemy. The aircraft carrier, was a relatively new weapon, which was extremely suited to hit and run warfare. The carriers themselves were extremely vulnerable, but they were capable of inflicting heavy punishment on their enemy from a very long range, as long as they could find him and strike first. As such, from a tactical perspective, it was imperative that an aircraft carrier keep moving; keep her scouts in the air searching for the enemy, flying wide search patterns; look for bad weather to hide yourself in so that your flight decks could not be easily spotted while at the same time pinning down your enemy in an area of clear visibility so that your planes can have an unrestricted attack on him. As Captain Sherman of the USS *Lexington* remarked, 'If they can't find you they can't hit you. The carrier is a weapon that can dash in, hit hard, and then disappear'.

Naval strategies started to develop around the support and defence of these colossal ships. Rather than a fleet of large gunned battleships travelling in convoys, the carriers were supported by ships designed to protect them from air attack with a large number of anti-aircraft guns aboard the other vessels supporting the throng already on the carrier. Destroyers would also be in the flotilla to offer anti-aircraft as well as anti-submarine support, and to perform the important task of rescuing downed airmen who, often after completing their own missions against enemy ships, would return to find their own carrier ablaze or sinking, being forced to ditch in the sea and hope for a rescue.

BATTLE OF THE CORAL SEA

N ow that the decision had been made by Japan not to invade Australia, due largely to supply constraints and the sheer size of the place, the question remained how to isolate it, and more importantly prevent it from becoming a staging post for the United States to springboard their way back into the Japanese conquered territories.

Instead, the Japanese would launch an offensive in the New Guinea – New Britain – Solomon Islands area. The Allies were aware through intelligence that such an attack was likely to take place and estimated that the enemy force might include five carriers, one battleship, five heavy cruisers, at least four light cruisers, 12 destroyers, and more than a dozen submarines. On top of this, perhaps 135 land based naval bombers, more than 100 Zeros and a similar number of reconnaissance planes. More than 20,000 troops could be brought into the theatre of battle in army transports. Further intelligence and naval plotting concluded that Port Moresby was the target. To the Allies, Port Moresby was far too strategically important a target to yield to the Japanese. It would provide the Japanese with a launching platform to commence attacks on air bases and ports in Queensland. It would enable Japan to extend air search patterns over the Coral Sea. It would enable a build-up of forces for the planned offensive to the east against New Caledonia, Fiji and Samoa. And although the Japanese had now ruled out an invasion of Australia for the time being, occupation of Port Moresby might effectively do the same thing, severing the great Island continent by effectively placing a noose around its neck. From a Port Moresby base, the great battleships and battlecruisers of the Japanese navy could patrol up and down the east coast of Australia keeping the country subjugated to their will.

General MacArthur stationed a bomber squadron in northern Queensland which started searching the Coral Sea to the east of Australia trying to spot the enemy convoy. It would comprise three fleets: the invasion force of soldiers for Port Moresby and the Solomons; two aircraft carriers from the Pearl Harbour attack (the Shokaka and the Suikaka) as a support contingent; and two heavy cruisers, a smaller carrier and supporting craft. As it turned out, the Japanese had 12 troop transports and 51 warships to protect them.

The Allies were able to field a naval force of only 20 vessels, however, these did include the two American aircraft carriers, the Yorktown and the Lexington. The Lexington was one of the largest aircraft carriers in the world and she was tenderly referred to by her crew as 'Lady Lex'. The ensuing fight between the two forces would become the first naval engagement in history ever fought without the opposing sides making visual contact.

Australia contributed a significant presence to the Allied force, which consisted of a heavy cruiser, HMAS *Australia*, and a light cruiser, HMAS *Hobart*. In addition, Australian air crews operated alongside the Americans out of the north Queensland air bases.

The battle got off to a good start for the Japanese when early in the morning on 7 May 1942, a US destroyer, *Sims,* and an oil tanker, *Neosho,* were sunk by Japanese planes. The *Sims* was hit by three bombs and sank immediately. Only 14 out of her 192-man crew survived. The *Neosho* was hit by seven bombs, and a Japanese dive bomber, which had been hit by anti-aircraft fire crashed into the oiler. A few hours later, around noon, American search aircraft spotted the carrier *Shoho* and a light cruiser which was escorting her. Although the *Shoho* was protected by 6 Zero fighter planes, the rest of her aircraft were below deck being prepared for attack against the American carriers. Planes from the *Yorktown* and the *Lexington* attacked and both vessels were sunk.

In the early afternoon, Japanese bombers attacked Allied ships in the formation led by Admiral Sir John Crace, which included the Australian ships as well as the US cruiser *Chicago*, and the US destroyers *Perkins, Walker* and *Farragut*. Crace was ready for an attack and the Allied formation countered with a powerful barrage of anti-aircraft fire hitting at least five of the bombers. The six remaining planes were unable to deliver a knockout blow to the Allies. The attack, which was over in less than 10 minutes and killed three Americans plus six Australians, in fact failed to severely damage any of the ships.

Shortly after this first attack, the Japanese attacked again with pattern bombing from high altitudes. Although the ships were drenched from the waves caused by the bombs exploding in the ocean, all survived. Crace managed to extricate his ships from the area in the night and avoided damage again from some US B17 bombers, which mistakenly had identified the ships as Japanese and attempted to sink them.

That evening, as the commander of the Japanese forces, Vice Admiral Inoue, poured over his charts and reflected on the outcome of the days operations, he decided to delay his invasion of Port Moresby by two days.

On 8 May at around 0800 hours both sides located the other's carriers. A pilot from the *Lexington* spotted the Japanese carriers *Shokaku* and *Zuikaku* through a break in the clouds, whilst about 390 kilometres away a spotter plane from the *Shokaku* spotted the US carriers and notified its position. Each side raced to launch their strike aircraft. At 0915 hours the Japanese launched a strike force of 18 fighters, 33 dive bombers and 18 torpedo planes. At 0925 hours the *Yorktown* and *Lexington* launched a joint force of 15 fighters, 39 dive bombers and 21 torpedo planes. Both carrier warship task forces immediately turned after launching their planes and headed straight towards each other at high speed in order to reduce the distance the aircraft would have to fly after completing their missions.

The planes from the *Yorktown* arrived first at 1057 hours and attacked the *Shokaku*. They hit the carrier with two 450 kg bombs causing heavy damage to the carrier's flight and hangar decks. None of the torpedo planes managed to hit the target. At 1130 hours, planes from the *Lexington* arrived and secured a further hit on the *Shokaku* with another 450 kg bomb. Other bombers attacked *Zuikaku*, however, failed to land a hit. The *Shokaku's* flight deck was badly damaged and 223 of her crew were killed or wounded. She requested permission to withdraw from the battle and this was given. At 1210 hours, accompanied by two destroyers, she retired from the scene.

While this was going on, the Japanese planes were launching attacks of their own. At 1113 hours they attacked the *Lexington* and the *Yorktown*. The initial four torpedos launched at *Yorktown* all missed; however, the remaining torpedo bombers formed a pincer attack on the *Lexington*, which, due to her size had a much larger turning radius, and successfully hit her with two torpedos.

Following the torpedo attack, the 33 dive bombers began their own attacks; 19 of them targeted *Lexington* while 14 targeted *Yorktown*. The *Lexington* was hit by two bombs that caused major damage and the *Yorktown* was hit in the centre of her flight deck by a 250 kg bomb which penetrated four decks below before exploding, causing severe damage to the ship and killing or wounding 66 of the American crew. Running low on fuel, the Japanese planes withdrew, believing that they had inflicted fatal damage to both carriers. On the way back to their respective carriers, planes from the two opposing forces passed each other in the sky and despite some minor skirmishes, the lack of fuel prevented an all-out aerial dogfight.

Whilst the *Yorktown* was able to limp away from the battle scene, the damage to the *Lexington* was too severe and the ship was ablaze. The captain gave the order for the crew to abandon their beloved 'Lady Lex' and more than 2,700 sailors were rescued. The USS *Phelps* was given the unpleasant job of sinking the *Lexington* with a torpedo to avoid it being salvaged by the Japanese.

By 9 May the Battle of the Coral Sea had come to an end after only a few days confrontation with substantial losses on both sides. The Allies had had one carrier destroyed and another crippled, one oiler and one destroyer sunk, 66 aircraft lost, and 543 men killed or wounded. The Japanese lost a carrier and had one crippled, three other naval ships and a destroyer were also sunk, 77 aircraft were lost, and 1074 men killed or wounded. Naturally, both Japan and the United States claimed 'victory' but the battle was quite even. In reality though, this was the first major defeat that the Japanese suffered in the war. Not so much in the battle itself but more what they failed to achieve as a result of the stalemate. The Americans, with their Australian Allies had prevented a landing and occupation at Port Moresby and the position of strength that this would have provided to the Imperial Japanese forces. More importantly, this potent war machine, which had been sweeping all before it since the early morning raid on Pearl Harbour could be defeated. When the morale of the Allies had been at its lowest point, the Imperial Forces had been shown to be no longer invincible.

Japanese aircraft preparing for action.

Japanese carrier *Shokaku* under attack
in the Battle of the Coral Sea.

THE LADY LEX

The *Lexington*, lovingly known by her crew as 'Lady Lex' was one of the largest, also the oldest, aircraft carriers in the world. Carrier aviation was still at its genesis in 1925, the year that she was launched. She was originally built as a battle cruiser, along with her sister, the *Saratoga*, but was converted to an aircraft carrier when her hull was finished. Her 36,000 tonne displacement was enormous when compared to the Enterprise, Hornet or Yorktown, all of which displaced less than 20,000 tonnes. She was around 70 feet longer than all of them and in addition she had a smaller island, leaving her with an extensive flight deck.

Although seafaring superstitions were largely a thing of the past, sailors held quirky feelings about the various ships in the US fleet, and the 'Lady Lex' always had a special place in their hearts. A sailor that served on her, Alvin Kernan, stated, 'The *Lexington* was a good ship, as was said in the navy, while her sister ship, the *Saratoga*, was not for unknown reasons.'

Accompanied by her escorts, the heavy cruisers Minneapolis and New Orleans, as well as seven destroyers, the *Lexington* left Pearl Harbour on 15 April 1942. She was fitted out with the latest in radar technology following her two-week sojourn in Pearl Harbour while refitting. Morale was boosted amongst the crew with the fitting of the radar as it gave them an added feeling of security and a sense of being less vulnerable to nasty surprises.

As the *Lexington* travelled towards the equatorial doldrums on its way to the Coral Sea, the sun radiated its muggy heat into the ship. Below the decks, the temperature hovered around 38 degrees Celsius during the day and did not fall below 32, even at night. Deep in the bowels of the ship, the *Lexington's* huge power plant included 16 large steam boilers and four 32,200 kilowatt turbine engines. A scorching heat was an inevitable by-product of such machinery and most of the heat remained trapped within the carrier's interior. During the heat of the day on the flight deck, when the heat from below merged with the equatorial sun from above, the deck plates were like frying pans and sailors would sometimes amuse themselves by frying eggs on them. The engine room itself was the hottest place on the ship and the engineers (also known as the black gang) worked away in an environment which never fell below 43 degrees Celsius and on occasion reached 55, which is about the upper limit of human endurance. Sailors who complained about the heat in the mess hall or on the hangar deck were often ordered by their superiors to go and pay a 'courtesy call' to the engineers, an experience that very quickly put their complaints into perspective. One sailor who 'visited' the black gang felt his 'eyeballs hardening like over-boiled eggs' and after a few hideous minutes he escaped back to the 'chilly upper world' where the temperature of 38 degrees Celsius felt very mild by comparison.

While at Pearl Harbour, the *Lexington* had had her 8 inch guns removed realising that these were relics of a past era when it was assumed that the ship may have exchanged fire with other ships. The reality is that these guns, which were mounted either side of the island, would only have been able to be fired to starboard. Had they been turned and fired to port, the muzzle blasts would have damaged the flight deck. It was becoming more apparent even at this early stage of the war that what was needed by all ships was more anti-aircraft weaponry. These large guns were replaced with several batteries of 38 calibre (5 inch) dual purpose guns on the bow and stern of the ship. These guns were very powerful and when handled by a skilled crew, they could knock down a heavy bomber travelling as high as 10,000 feet above the ship. On top of these, in excess of a hundred shorter range guns, 1.1 inch and 20 mm Oerlikons, were spread all around the perimeter of the flight deck. Although they were fairly ineffective at long range, they could be fired very rapidly by a man strapped into the shoulder braces making them useful for last ditch defence against an oncoming plane.

As the 'Lady Lex' approached the equator the crew prepared for the traditional 'crossing the line' ceremony. The ships company was divided into the 'shellbacks' – old salts that had crossed the line before, and the 'pollywogs' – those who had not. For 24 hours the pollywogs were subjected to various rituals while the shellbacks imposed a reign of terror upon them as they were initiated into the domain of *Neptunus Rex*. It was generally a period of high hilarity where tensions were released, and the veterans could flex their muscles against the new recruits of which about 500-odd had not yet even been to sea before. At all times though during the crossing the line ceremony, the ships battle readiness was never relaxed.

Air patrols continued to take off and half the crew always remained at their stations. The new recruits were brought before 'Neptune's Court' during the ceremony where they were asked insulting and preposterous questions and no matter how they answered they were likely to be held in contempt of court. The pollywogs were allowed to attempt to bribe the court with Coca-Cola, ice cream or cigarettes. If any of them testified that they had served in military intelligence they were immediately convicted of perjury on the basis that no such thing had ever existed. Rookie pilots were required to spend the day in the tropical heat in fur lined jackets with gloves and helmets, scanning the tropical horizon for icebergs using binoculars made from a pair of coke bottles.

In the afternoon the ceremony ended on the forward of the flight deck where King Neptune (usually a long serving officer) sat on a throne wearing a crown and holding a trident. He was flanked by his 'queen' and a 'royal baby'. The pollywogs were stripped to their underwear and anointed (painted) with a foul concoction of torpedo grease and banana oil and whatever other disgusting items could be scrounged from the machine shops or the galley. Following King Neptune's benediction, the painted pollywogs were ordered to run the gauntlet down the flight deck one at a time whilst the whole time being smashed on the buttocks by several hundred shellbacks. On reaching the end, he received a certificate stating that he had officially entered King Neptune's domain and now he was an official shellback.

The blue shirts and dungarees of the *Lexington's* crew were soaked through within minutes of being put on such was the humidity of the tropics. In these days before deodorants became popular, or available, they were plagued by the stench of their own, as well as other, bodies. They could shower as often as they felt like it, but they were salt water showers with a very brief freshwater rinse, plus the bottom of the washrooms collected three or four inches of oil and soapy water which sloshed from side to side with the rolling of the ship meaning that the legs and feet never really got clean. They shaved in salt water creating a toll on their skin and every man on the ship suffered heat rash, particularly below the waistline where sweat soaked underwear chafed at the skin causing welts to develop to the height of over an inch and were red raw. Few men could sleep in the heat and there was a constant stream of men back and forward to the heads in the red glare of the night lights. Many sought refuge from the heat on the flight deck, battling each other for a spot in the bomb nets which were quite comfortable with a blanket placed across the wire for padding. With the breeze generated by the forward momentum of the ship, it became quite pleasant after midnight.

On 19 April the *Lexington* received orders from Nimitz to proceed towards New Caledonia and intercept with the *Yorktown*, join Task Force 17 and proceed toward the Coral Sea. On 8 May, after entering the Battle of the Coral Sea, the enormous carrier was to meet her doom. After offloading her own aircraft to inflict damage against the Japanese, she was struck by Japanese torpedo bombers and then again, by the dive bombers shortly after. The damage that she sustained was too great and the fires deep inside of the ship caused explosions to happen for hours afterwards causing her steel hull to twist and buckle. After her surviving crew had been evacuated, the USS *Phelps* arrived on the scene to commit the coupe de grace and send the 'Lady Lex' to the bottom of the ocean.

So beloved was this carrier that news of her demise caused flags to be flown at half-mast in Washington, and at CINPAC (Commander in Chief Pacific Fleet Headquarters) in Hawaii where Admiral Chester Nimitz announced the loss of the *Lexington*. A memorial to the ship, which includes the ship's bell which was retrieved prior to her sinking, currently stands in Massachusetts in the town that bears her name.

Crew abandon the *Lexington*
during the battle of the coral sea.

USS *Lexington* firing 203mm guns.

American forces preparing for an invasion.

THE PACIFIC CAMPAIGN
CONTINUES

A lthough the Battle of the Coral Sea may not have been a convincing Allied victory, with both sides coming out of it about evenly, it did have the effect nonetheless of temporarily halting the advance of the Japanese Imperial Forces and for the time being put paid to any designs for an invasion and occupation of Australia. The war in the Pacific would, however, continue for over three more years before the Japanese surrender to the Allied forces, in Tokyo Bay, during August 1945.

In that three and a half years the Allies would inflict many defeats against Japan, as they slowly and painstakingly gained the upper hand and crept towards the Japanese mainland. And all the time the Japanese forces doggedly held on, allowing these victories to be achieved only at great cost to the Allies.

The Australian victory on the Kokoda track in Papua New Guinea, comprehensive American victories at Midway Island,

Guadalcanal, Iwo Jima, Okinawa to name a few, crushed the Japanese Air Force, Army and Navy before American forces were poised to invade the main islands of Japan, prior to the dropping of the atomic bombs and the ending of the war. The loss of Japan's best aircraft carriers early in the war at Midway, and the Japanese High Command's belief in the big guns of battleships, supplemented by air support from carriers along with light cruisers and destroyers, would have significant consequences. The forward thinking of the US navy that the carrier was the modern superweapon, with the ability to send its airplanes hundreds of kilometres beyond the range of battleship guns, would prove decisive. On top of this, the sheer scale of American industrial might by comparison to Japan would prove the most significant factor and guarantee the final victory. The United States Navy started World War II with seven aircraft carriers, but another 160 were built over the course of the war and by 1945, with its industrial machine fully geared towards the military, it was capable of building 100 new ships per year. By comparison, Japan commenced the war with 10 modern aircraft carriers but after The Battle of Midway in 1942 did not produce a single one more.

The dropping of the atomic bombs on Japan was not a decision that was made lightly. But by that time the people of the United States were weary of war. Germany had surrendered in May 1945 and the Victory in Europe celebrations were almost a distant memory. The battle for the Island of Okinawa, only 550 kilometres from mainland Japan lasted 82 days from 1 April to 22 June. The capture of Okinawa was essential as it was planned to be the staging area for the eventual invasion of Japan that was to occur in

November 1945. The Americans suffered 75,000 casualties and Japan more than 120,000 during the battle. In addition, 149,425 Okinawans were killed or committed suicide in the fighting. This was a significant proportion of the estimated pre-war population of 300,000.

It was clear that if the Japanese were going to fight so hard for Okinawa, they would fight equally hard, if not harder to defend their homeland when the Americans finally invaded. The invasion of Japan, codenamed Operation Downfall, was to involve two separate amphibious landings; one on the Southern Japanese Island of Kyushu, and the other near Tokyo, on the main Island of Honshu. Following the ferocity of the Battle of Okinawa, President Truman and his advisers estimated that American losses could exceed 500,000 in the Battle for Japan with significantly more Japanese losses. The threat of wholesale Japanese civilian suicide, following the Okinawan experience, also weighed heavily on their minds.

The US navy urged the use of a blockade and airpower to bring about Japan's submission and to postpone the invasion of the mainland to 1947 or 1948, however, the American Joint Chiefs of Staff felt that prolonging the war to such an extent would be dangerous for national morale. With the war in Europe over, and a public longing to 'bring the boys home', this assumption was correct. Russia's recent intervention in to the Pacific War with the invasion of Manchuria and its own designs on the expansion of its empire into the Pacific also gave the Allies cause for concern. This was doubly concerning for America given that tensions were now arising between the Russians and the British and Americans in Europe. As well as ending the war against

Japan more quickly by using the bombs, America could send a very clear message to the Soviet Union about its newfound technological superiority with their deployment.

Total military losses in the Pacific War were immense. Japan suffered heavily, with 1,740,000 army, navy and air force personnel killed. They had a relatively small number wounded, 94,000, and even fewer taken as prisoners of war, at 42,000. The low number of wounded and POW's reflected the Japanese willingness to literally fight to the death, and their belief that being taken as a prisoner was dishonourable. The United States suffered 112,000 deaths, 255,000 wounded and 21,500 POW's. Australia had 9,470 military deaths, 14,000 wounded and 22,000 prisoners of war. The United Kingdom suffered 5,670 military dead, 12,840 wounded and 50,000 prisoners. Most of the Australian and British POW's were taken at the fall of Singapore. They were sent to the notorious Changi prison or to work on the Burma railway. In both of those locations many of them were to die.

Civilian deaths during the Pacific War were horrendous. China, who had suffered occupation at the hands of the Japanese since 1932 had 18,000,000 civilians killed, along with 4,000,000 Chinese soldiers. India suffered 2,000,000 civilian deaths, Indonesia 4,000,000 and the Philippines 1,000,000. Japan suffered 400,000 civilian deaths, predominately at the hands of the strategic US bombing campaign, and the bombs dropped on Hiroshima and Nagasaki.

For the submarine personnel in Fremantle, little did they know just how significant their contribution to the final victory would be. In fact, when it was fully active, the base saw 170 Dutch, British and American submarines pass through the harbour. Many of these vessels had highly successful military campaigns and made a huge contribution to the Allied war effort. One of America's most successful submarines of World War II, the USS *Flasher,* conducted much of her operations from the Port of Fremantle. *Flasher* (SS-249) was a *Gato*-class submarine who was launched on 20 June 1943. She received the Presidential Unit Citation and six battle stars and sank 21 ships for a total of 100,231 tonnes of Japanese shipping.

For the people of Fremantle life went on over those remaining years and they were thankful in the end that the defences put in place to protect this vital port were never called into play to fight off an invading force. The gun batteries, from Rottnest Island to Swanbourne to Point Peron, never fired a shot in anger, but gave comfort to the local citizens, who were aware of the importance of their port city to the Allied war effort, yet never fully aware of the true contribution of Fremantle to the outcome of the Pacific War and World War II.

Raising the flag on Iwo Jima.

REFERENCES

Pacific 360 - Roland Perry

Kokoda - Peter Fitzsimons

Pacific Crucible - Ian W. Toll

Retribution - Max Hastings

Japan's Longest Day - Compiled by the Pacific War
    Research Society

The Admirals - Walter R. Borneman

The Battle for Singapore - Peter Thomson

The Battleships - Ian Johnston and Rob McAuley

Inferno - Max Hastings

The Second World War - Antony Beevor

Defending Fremantle, Albany and Bunbury 1939-1945 -
    Graham McKenzie Smith

US Navy Aircraft Carriers 1922-1945 - Mark Stille

When the War Came to Fremantle 1899 to 1945 -
    Deborah Gare and Madison Lloyd Jones

ABOUT THE AUTHOR

Tim Baldock is an avid military historian, with *Fortress Fremantle: Its Lost Sub & Contribution to World War II* being his first book on the subject. The decision to write about the Pacific War was driven by his personal interest in that campaign, largely influenced through his work as a volunteer tour guide on Rottnest Island in Western Australia where the Oliver Hill Gun Battery still stands today.

A proud West Australian, who grew up with a deep connection to Fremantle, this book has allowed him to share his passion for history with his love of the Port.

 **Follow Tim on Facebook**
@reflectionsofmilitaryhistory

CPSIA information can be obtained
at www.ICGtesting.com
Printed in the USA
LVHW080012060421
683517LV00016B/1091